The
Asymptote
of Love

The
Asymptote
of Love

From Mundane
to Religious
to God's Love

James Kellenberger

Cover photo of the California desert taken by the author

Revised Standard Version of the Bible, copyright 1952 (2nd ed., 1971) by the Division of Christian Education of the National Council of Churches of Christ in the United States of America. Used by permission. All rights reserved.

Published by State University of New York Press, Albany

For information, contact State University of New York Press, Albany, NY
www.sunypress.edu

Library of Congress Cataloging-in-Publication Data

Names: Kellenberger, James, author.
Title: The asymptote of love : from mundane to religious to God's love / James
  Kellenberger.
Description: Albany : State University of New York, 2018. | Includes bibli-
  ographical references and index.
Identifiers: LCCN 2017058362| ISBN 9781438471778 (hardcover : alk. paper) |
  ISBN 9781438471792 (e-book) | ISBN 9781438471785 (paperback : alk. paper)
Subjects: LCSH: Love—Religious aspects. | Love. | God—Love. | God—Worship
  and love.
Classification: LCC BL626.4 .K45 2018 | DDC 205/.677—dc23 LC record
  available at https://lccn.loc.gov/2017058362

10 9 8 7 6 5 4 3 2 1

TO ANNE

CONTENTS

ACKNOWLEDGMENTS

I am grateful to my wife Anne for suggestions regarding the title of this book, to Christopher Ahn for his editorial advice and support, and to Diane Ganeles for her attentive care in guiding the book through production.

At several points I have used material from my *Relationship Morality* (Pennsylvania State University Press, 1995), which has been adapted to the discussion in this book and is used with permission.

Introduction

AFTER CONSIDERING SEVERAL ALTERNATIVES for this book's title I settled first on *The Asymptote of Love*, and then with editorial encouragement on *The Asymptote of Love: From Mundane to Religious to God's Love*. The title is descriptive. This book is indeed about the asymptote of love. An asymptote is a line that approaches a point, ever drawing nearer, but reaching its endpoint only at infinity. The asymptote of love reaches toward the infinite endpoint of love, love at its uttermost, the zenith of love, God's love in theistic traditions. In writing the book I discovered that Leo Tolstoy had used the image of the asymptote in a related application in his *The Kingdom of God Is Within You*, where he said, "Divine perfection is the asymptote of the human life." Tolstoy's reflections on Christianity will come into our discussion, although what Tolstoy understands as an asymptote of the human life toward divine perfection differs from the asymptote of love. Still, his trope of the asymptote, which approaches its ideal in an infinite journey, ever drawing nearer as it approaches its ideal, serves well the premise of our discussion and coincides with the intended meaning of this book's title. The asymptote of love ascends from quotidian and even mundane love to religious love and God's love and approaches love at its infinite, its zenith, its uttermost, God's love in a theistic understanding.

The idea of uttermost love owes much to religion, in particular to Christianity, in which God is love, but not to Christianity alone. We are called on to love or to have compassion in more than one religious tradition, and the traditions of several religions will be consulted as we seek an understanding of uttermost love. Also we will consult authors who speak from outside religion, some of whom are negatively disposed toward religion and some of whom are not. Their critical perspectives will augment the religious sources that we draw on and will help us to consider issues and possibilities relevant to the nature of uttermost love and the form of love that begins to approach it.

The nature of love as a general concept, along with the range of expressions of love, is a preliminary part of our subject. In pursuing it we will address what in a sense we already know. It is a paradox of intellectual or philosophical reflection going back to Plato and his teacher Socrates that in asking what the nature of love is (or knowledge or beauty), as Socrates did, we pose a question using a term that we are already familiar with and use with comparative ease. Moreover, if we proceed to proffer an analysis or account of, say, knowledge, we can test that analysis or account using our pretheoretical understanding. While there may be a point to complaining to someone "You don't know what love is!" it remains that speakers of natural languages have *love* (or *amour* or *Liebe*, etc.) in their vocabularies.

So we may already have a grasp of the nature of love implicitly, without being able to articulate its nature, not fully. Yet knowing its nature in this way, and even being able to distinguish expressions of genuine love from expressions of false love, is not yet to know the zenith of love. It is not in itself being able to trace the asymptote of love in its approach to infinite uttermost love.

Uttermost love is love. But love, as we will remind ourselves in chapter 1, can be of many different things and have many different emotional shadings. The form of love that is our subject will emerge over the extended course of our discussion. It can be said at this point, however, that uttermost love, in its concept, is rooted in religious sensibility and tradition. If we allow a religious grounding of uttermost love in the Jewish and Christian traditions, it would not be wrong to think of love of God and of neighbor as significant parts of uttermost love or of love that approaches uttermost love. Yet doing so is but an initial step, for the character and demands of that love are not disclosed thereby. Furthermore uttermost love has a possibly fuller range that is not captured in the Christian and Jewish commands.

As we pursue our discussion we will at various points encounter concerns and issues. Some will relate to love in its general concept; some will relate to religious love; some will relate to understanding God's love as uttermost love; and some will relate to the nature and scope of love that begins to approach uttermost love. Some of these concerns, though not all, will be raised by religious writers and thinkers from within a religious tradition, especially Christianity. Some will be raised by those whose reflections are not religiously grounded.

IN CHAPTER 1, as we have indicated, we will look at the range of love's varieties and types; and we will see how love is a multifarious concept that resists an essentialist definition.

Love is relational, but it can be embodied in many different relationships. In chapter 2, we will give attention to interpersonal forms of love, especially romantic love, and offer initial reflections on two forms of religious love that can seem problematic, proper self-love and love of God. The thesis that love bestows value, as opposed to responding to the one who is loved and that person's value, will be examined; and two issues that relate to love in general and religious love in particular will be recognized and introduced—the issue of love's rationality, grounded in modern thinking, and the older issue of the place in love of self-denial.

In chapter 3, which is on the love of others, we will turn our attention to religious love of one's neighbors, one of the book's major themes. How one is to love one's neighbors is, in the Christian tradition, contained in the teachings of the New Testament, and we will consult some of these, including the parable of the Good Samaritan, to bring into relief how religious love of one's neighbors is at variance with the requirements of conventional morality. Also in this chapter, drawing on a particular religious sensibility, we will introduce the theme of loving God through loving others.

Some have posited a connection between knowing God and loving God that makes them identical: to know God is to love God. There are questions, though, about this thesis, including a question about the nature of the knowledge of God that is to be identical with love of God. An examination of this thesis and its issues is the subject of chapter 4.

In the Jewish and Christian traditions there are two great commandments to love. One is to love God with all one's heart and soul, and the other is to love one's neighbors as oneself. Immanuel Kant, though, challenged the idea that there can be a command or duty to love, as opposed to a duty to do good for others. Even some more clearly within the Christian tradition have raised a question about the command to love if it commands us to have the *feeling* of love, as it arguably does. These concerns will be treated in chapter 5.

The subject of chapter 6 is love of God, another major theme of this book. Here we will consider the question of whether love of God, or of neighbor, can be purely a response to a duty to follow a command, and we will note how medieval monastics thought it necessary to designate "signs" of genuine love of God. In this chapter we will also attend to the expressions of love of God identified by St. Bernard of Clairvaux and St. Francis de Sales. Some have spoken of loving others "in God" or "for the sake of God," and these significant but opaque religious categories will be addressed in chapter 6.

Chapter 7 has as its subject God's love. It too is a central theme of this book. For theistic religions God's love is the highest form of love. It is the zenith of love and in this book's terms it is the infinite endpoint of the asymptote of love. But how is it known? And can it be known? Both of these questions will be addressed, drawing on two divergent religious sensibilities and two different theological approaches with which they are correlated, one the apophatic approach of Dionysius, the other the theology of St. Thomas Aquinas. Different Christian images of God's love will be presented, which point a way toward an experience of God's love. And in the chapter's final section Buddhist analogues of God's love and a devotional Hindu image of God's love will be brought forward.

One question regarding uttermost love and a religious love that begins to approach it regards the scope of love. What is included in the circle of such love? In chapter 8 this question will be taken up. Religious love of neighbor is universal, but how can distant strangers, never seen, be loved? And beyond God and human beings does the circle of religious love include other beings of the earth?

In chapter 8 the scope of religious love is considered; in chapter 9 its complement, the depth of religious love, is considered. The depth of religious love, as for all love, importantly involves love's interior dimension. An integral part of the interior depth of religious love is loss of self, and the character of religious love's loss of self will be examined. However, the interior dimension of religious love can be given a disproportionate stress, it will be argued, and two instances of this will be discussed.

Chapter 10, whose chapter title is the book's title, considers God's love, the endpoint of the asymptote of love, in its role as an infinite ideal of love, at once unattainable and directive. Chapter 10, along with chapters 8 and 9, attempts to address the character of uttermost love or religious love that begins to approach it, as much as it is knowable. Compassion, so important for Buddhism, is compared with Christian love, or *agape*, and their interconnectedness will be traced. Chapter 10 returns to the issue of love's reasonableness, but reintroduces it as a question about appropriateness as it relates to religious love. In this chapter it is shown how, for at least some religious sensibilities, religious love is appropriately given to the beings of the earth and given as the beings loved deserve. In the chapter's final section a recapitulation of the book's themes and concerns is provided.

Often the themes of this book that are introduced in one chapter will be returned to and enlarged in another. The theme of God's love and how it might be known, for instance, is introduced in chapter 7 and returned to in chapter 9. Some important themes run through the book as threads run through a fabric. One of these is the theme of the multiple connections between God's love and human love. The major themes of God's love and human religious love run through many of the book's chapters because many of the book's other themes, such as the scope of religious love, reflect back on them.

Chapter One

The Varieties of Love

I. INTRODUCTION

OUR CONCERN IN THIS BOOK is with the asymptote of love that approaches uttermost love, love at its zenith. As love, uttermost love is in a class or family. In this first chapter we will introduce that family in its phenomenological vastness.

In section II we will remind ourselves of the range of things that can be loved, the wide range of the objects of human love, and we will also note the affective shading in different instances of love.

In section III we will observe how love can be divided into different types. In fact there are several ways to divide love into different types, as we will see. Though there are various classifications of love, all or many of these divisions are natural in that they appeal to recognizable characteristics of love to define its different types. Each division divides love into natural types, we may say. Love is less like a cake and more like an orange. A cake can be cut into four, ten, or twenty pieces, as we arbitrarily please. An orange has segments that naturally divide it. The analogy is not perfect, for love, unlike an orange, can be naturally divided in more than one way, using different principal attributes to define its segments.

Section IV offers reflections on the kind of concept love is. Love, it will be argued, resists an essentialist definition.

II. LOVE IN ITS MULTIPLICITY

THE WORD *love* is used to describe the closest and most intimate of human relationships. Love animates marital relationships when they are realized in their potential. We recognize and expect a presence of love in parent-child and

1

brother-sister relationships. Friends love one another. Also, though, we love ice cream, travel, a good meal, and sports. One may love one's job or oneself. One may love doing good in gratitude or doing evil in revenge, or both. Some of the Romantic poets are said to have been in love with love. And one may love God. There is a nearly limitless variety in the range of the objects of love. When we turn our attention to the affective side of these different instances of love, even if we limit our attention to the more familiar instances of love, we find a range of sentiments that may be prominent: enjoyment (ice cream), appreciation and satisfaction (one's job), or emotional engagement and deep affection (one's beloved).

The multiplicity of love is not a phenomenon of the English language. It is to be found in French where *j'aime* is used to express one's love of another person, sports, a good meal, or God, and in German where *Ich liebe* is used to express one's love of the same range of objects. The same range is found in other languages as well.

III. TYPES OF LOVE

WITH LITTLE EFFORT we can designate different types of love. We can, for instance, distinguish different types of love on the basis of love's different objects, so that love of a good meal is one kind of love and love of sports is another. Using this principle of classification we would generate a nearly infinite number of types of love. As Mike Martin observes, "we can love all kinds of things," and limiting himself to the letter *p* he names as possible objects of love "painting, parties, peace, peaches, penguins, people, perfumes, piccolos, places, poetry, and power."[1] If, on the other hand, we look to the nature of the love that is given, as opposed to love's object, we would identify other types of love. Following this approach we might identify selfish love and unselfish love, or among other types romantic love and transactional love (love

---

1   Mike Martin, *Love's Virtues* (Lawrence KS: University Press of Kansas, 1996), p. 12. Martin names these as things that might be loved using a meaning of love that he proposes, which we will turn to shortly.

given for reciprocation). Joseph Runzo, using two Greek words for love, *agape* and *eros*, identifies "seraphic love," in which there is "the unity of *eros*," understood as active and passionate love, "and *agape*," understood as altruistic love.[2]

There are four Greek words for love: *agape* for altruistic love, *eros* for yearning love, *philia* for the love of friendship, and *storge* for affectionate family love. These Greek terms in effect name four different kinds of love and so in themselves provide yet another classification of the types of love. Its use goes back to antiquity, and a brief comment on the types of love it names is in order.

Agape is the Greek word most often used for love in the New Testament. It is altruistic love, willed and freely given without a requirement of reciprocation. *Agape* in the New Testament is the love Christians should have for God and for their neighbors, and *agape* is the word used for God's love for us. The usual Latin word for *agape* is *caritas*, and it is sometimes translated in English as *charity* (in its New Testament sense). In fact the King James Bible sometimes translates the Greek *agape* as *charity*, as it does when Paul in his First Letter to the Corinthians places *agape* above faith and hope (1 Cor. 13.13). By contrast, the Revised Standard Version (RSV) translates *agape* as love, so that the verse in Paul's First Letter to the Corinthians reads: "faith, hope, love, abide, these three; but the greatest of these is love."[3]

Eros is passionate and active. It is that love which yearns or longs for what will fulfill it. *Eros* clearly is to be found in romantic love, and as romantic love it has often been given poetic expression. When one "falls in love" the love is *eros* in its romantic or erotic expression. One does not "fall in" or into *agapeistic* love. However, *eros* need not be erotic. It need not be sexual or sensual. In Plato's *Symposium*, in Socrates's presentation, love is the love of, the longing for, beauty first as it is found in physical things and then in the virtues, and

---

2   Joseph Runzo, "Eros and Meaning in Life and Religion," in *The Meaning of Life in the World Religions*, ed. Joseph Runzo and Nancy M. Martin (Oxford: Oneworld, 2000), pp. 194–95.

3   All biblical quotations are from the RSV unless otherwise indicated.

finally, climbing the "heavenly ladder, stepping from rung to rung," the aspirant will come to a contemplation of "the beautiful itself."[4] For Plato, in its higher forms *eros* passes from love of the bodily and sensual to love of the moral and nonsensual. Independently of the *Symposium* we can recognize a yearning love of various objects.

The Greek *eros* is not used in the New Testament, apparently because in the first centuries of the Common Era *eros* was associated with the sensual. Nevertheless there are biblical instances of *eros*. A notable example is in Psalm 42:

> As a hart longs
>   for flowing streams,
>   so longs my soul
>   for thee, O God.

Within religion, but also outside religion, a love of virtue as a yearning to be virtuous accompanied by a moral striving would be a form of nonsensual *eros*.

Philia names the kind of love that is appropriate to friendship and to brotherly love. Aristotle (384–22 BCE) in his *Nicomachean Ethics* discusses friendship, which he regards as a "kind of virtue" or a relationship that "implies virtue," and the love found in friendship or *philia*.[5] Aristotle distinguishes several kinds of friendship, including a perfect form, which he apparently sees as existing between men. The marital relationship between a husband and wife he sees as a kind of friendship, but it is also "an aristocracy" in which the "man rules by virtue of merit."[6] Contrary to what Aristotle seems to think, there of course is no reason why women cannot be friends in the highest sense. In the New Testament *philia* is used to refer to brotherly love, as

---

4   Plato, *Symposium* 201a–12a, trans. Michael Joyce, in *The Collected Dialogues of Plato*, ed. Edith Hamilton and Huntington Cairns (Princeton, NJ: Princeton University Press, 1963), pp. 553–63.

5   Aristotle, *Nicomachean Ethics*, Bks. VIII and IX, 1155a3–72a15, in *The Ethics of Aristotle: The Nicomachean Ethics*, trans. J. A. K. Thomson and rev. Hugh Tredennick (New York: Penguin Books, 1976), pp. 258–311.

6   Aristotle, *Nicomachean Ethics*, Bk. VIII, 1160b16, p. 276.

when St. Paul says, "love one another with brotherly affection" (Rom. 12.10), which would apply to both women and men.

Storge is the love of family or family affection. Like *eros* the Greek word *storge* is not used in the New Testament. Still there are in the New Testament settings that embody the kind of love that *storge* names. One instance of this is in the book of John, in the story of Jesus bringing back to life Lazarus (Jn. 11). Lazarus is the brother of Mary and Martha. When he falls ill, Mary and Martha send for Jesus; and he comes to them, but only after staying two days more where he and his disciples were. When he arrives in the village of Mary and Martha he finds them distraught because Lazarus has died. "Lord, if you had been here," Martha says, "my brother would not have died," and Mary repeats these words. Jesus is deeply moved by their grief and calls Lazarus back to life from his tomb. Jesus loved Lazarus and Martha and Mary, we are told. What is to be noted here is not his love for them or the miracle of his raising Lazarus from death, but Jesus' acknowledgment of the sisters' love for their brother, which exemplifies family affection.[7]

IV. LOVE AS A MULTIFARIOUS CONCEPT

LOVE HAS MULTIPLE OBJECTS, and its affective constituent can vary as much as its object. If we limit our concern to love between persons it yet separates into distinguishable types. The four types corresponding to the four Greek words for love all apply to human relationships, even if two of the four, *agape* and *eros*, also apply more broadly. Love, so importantly represented in inter-personal relations, is not limited to human relations. Love may be of parties or peaches, of sports or fancy food. Love, moreover, can take various forms regarding its affect as much as its object. Love of fancy food is in its emotional content different from love of one's children, and love of one's children is in its expression different from love of one's parents. Love is in this way a

---

7   The four kinds of love that C. S. Lewis discusses in his *The Four Loves* (New York: Harcourt, Brace, and Company, 1960) correspond to these four. While he uses the Greek terms *eros*, *philia*, and *storge* for three of the main kinds of love he distinguishes, he uses *charity* rather than *agape* for the fourth type, and he understands it as love of God.

multifarious concept. It is, we may say, a polythetic concept, that is, a concept without a clear essentialist definition (consisting of necessary and sufficient conditions).The concept of love allows many ways of loving, having love, and being in love, as well as many different objects of love.

Nevertheless definitions of love have been offered. Baruch Spinoza (1632–77) defined love as "pleasure accompanied by the idea of an external cause." Other translations use *joy* rather than *pleasure*. By *idea* Spinoza here means *belief*.[8] Love one has for another person for Spinoza, then, on his definition is the pleasure or joy one has accompanied by the belief one has regarding that other person. Spinoza took his definition to be the "essence of love," but he allowed that it is one of the properties of love that the "lover wishes to be united to the object of his love" (other translations use "wills" in places of "wishes") provided we understand "wishes" (or "wills") to mean "the satisfaction" that the beloved object produces in the lover by its presence.[9] Mike Martin says that "'true love' refers to any strong positive attraction" and provides a definition of love or of what we truly love as "what most strongly attracts us," which, he says, allows that "we can love all kinds of things."[10] Both Spinoza and Martin, then, define love in terms of the emotional response of the one who loves.

There is something intuitive in thinking of love in terms of the pleasure or joy we feel in the presence of what or whom we love or in terms of the attraction we feel for what or whom we love. We naturally delight in the presence of those things, and especially those persons, we love, and we are naturally attracted to the things and persons we love. It is not clear, though, that these definitions are adequate as essentialist definitions. For one thing, since they designate different properties, if one is right the other cannot be.

---

8   Jonathan Bennett, *A Study of Spinoza's Ethics* (Indianapolis, IN: Hackett, 1984), p. 269.

9   Baruch Spinoza, *Ethics*, Part III Concerning the Origin and Nature of the Emotions, Definitions of the Emotions, in *Spinoza's Ethics*, trans. Andrew Boyle (London: Dent and New York: Dutton, 1959), p. 130.

10   Martin, *Loves's Virtues*, p. 12.

But moreover neither property seems to be sufficient in its presence for love while in its absence excluding all that is not love, as an essentialist definition is intended to do. If strong attraction were the same as love, and so sufficient for love, then there would be no cases of strong attraction that were not instances of love. But there are. Addicts are strongly attracted by the substance to which they are addicted, but they may not love the substance to which they are addicted. They may wish to be free of their habit. Those who are captivated by another person may be strongly attracted to that person without loving him or her; those who are merely infatuated with another person are strongly attracted to that person, though so far love has yet to emerge.

Spinoza defines love in terms of the pleasure or joy the one who loves has occasioned by the object of that love or one's thought of that object. Often of course human beings delight in what or whom they love, but this definition also is inadequate as an essentialist definition. It does not apply to agapeistic love in particular. Mother Teresa of Calcutta (Kolkata) was active and also at peace and joyful with the quiet joy of spiritual joy. But her love for the sick and those in need was not her joy, and it is misrepresentative to say that she took pleasure in helping others. Her love was more her concern and sympathy for others, rather than her pleasure or joy in helping them.

In chapter 2 we will argue that love is relational, that in instances of love there is the one who loves and the object of love, which may be a thing or person or God. These two, the subject who loves and the object that is loved, form a binary relationship. This relational property of love, though, does not provide us with an essentialist definition of love. It does not define love, for it is not love alone that has this relational property. Hate, for instance, does as well. Hate in the same way requires one who hates and that which is hated. And so too for jealousy, wanting to help, fear, and other examples. Also, as we will see and underline in later chapters, religious love, and all love in some degree, has both an interior and an exterior dimension, but again this dual aspect of love does not define love, or religious love, for this dual aspect is seen also in, for example, hate and jealousy and other emotional states.

Even if is there is not an essentialist definition that applies to all love, or applies only to all love of persons for other persons, love relationships can be distinguished from relationships or states that are superficially similar. Love can be distinguished from infatuation or liking another person (which may or may not accompany loving another person). It can be distinguished from the desire to help others or actually helping others (help may be given from a variety of motives, including the desire for approval or a sense of moral duty, although, of course, help can be given out of love). Love, even without an all-embracing definition, can be distinguished from antithetical states, such as hate and antipathy. Even without an essentialist definition, love can be distinguished from closely related states, such as when one feels respect for persons, just as it can be distinguished from compassion, which in its religious expression is closely related (in the final chapter we will discuss how love and compassion differ, and how they interdigitate).

Some may speak of "true love," but love in all its varieties is truly love, even loving to see one's enemies suffer. There are different ways to love things and other persons, but each is an expression of love. Some may mean by "true love" a more valuable form of love. This is different. Not all expressions of love are equally valuable. Some forms or expressions may be morally more valuable than others, or otherwise more valuable, and some may even be morally objectionable. Great love may be spoken of, meaning love that is of a great or passionate intensity, and some instances of love may be greater in other ways: more enduring or involving greater sacrifice. Ideal love may also be spoken of: humanly ideal love is love beyond the common run, to be sought after but perhaps never attained.

ALL THESE FORMS OF LOVE, from the trivial to the profound and the humanly ideal, are love. They in some way participate in the nature of love. All are distinguishable from uttermost love, that infinite love toward which the asymptote of love reaches, in theistic traditions God's love.

The asymptote of love is the subject of this book. The uttermost love that is infinitely approached is indeed love and by its nature is within the polythetic embrace of love's concept. But its form and expression will take some discovery, as will its character and ambit and the nature of love that begins to approach uttermost love.

Chapter Two

Love's Relationships

I. INTRODUCTION

LOVE IN ITS VARIOUS FORMS AND EXPRESSIONS is by its nature relational. In every instance of love there is one who loves and the object of that love. The basic or core relationship of love is binary, a two-place relationship between the one giving love and love's object. There are, however, many variants of love's binary relationship, some of which are trivial, as we have seen, and some of which, as exemplified by love between persons, that are profound. Variations among love's relationships will be the subject of section II of this chapter.

In section III. we will examine the idea that love of one person for another, especially in the form of romantic love, is an "emotional process."

Section IV addresses the question of whether love "bestows" value on the person who is loved. Does love *create* value in the one who is loved, or does love *find* value in the one who is loved?

In section V we will give attention to questions that have importance within philosophical reflection on love but also have traction for modernity and its mind-set: Is love rational? Is love reasonable?

Finally in section VI, the place of self-denial in love will be examined.

II. VARIANTS OF LOVE'S RELATIONSHIPS

ALWAYS WHEN THERE IS LOVE there is one who loves, the subject of love, and the person or thing loved, the object of love. Love in its various manifestations unavoidably has this binary character, although this basic binary relationship has variants that are significantly different.

9

We see the binary character of love in the mundane love for *things*, even in its trivial instances. Love for ice cream, a good meal, or travel manifests this character, as do deeper forms of love. We see it, for instance, in the love a person may have for a cherished pet. And it is present in the profound love that one person may have for another person. In the range of love between persons the character of the love that is given varies with the relationship, but the basic binary nature of love persists. Also, more significantly, the expressions of love and its very forms are different. The relationship formed by the love of friendship, though binary, is very different from love for a thing like ice cream or travel. One's love for a friend is richer and more multidimensional than love for a thing like ice cream, and it is more personal than love for a thing like travel. Moreover, the love one has for a friend in a friendship of any depth is returned by the friend. Typically in fully realized love relationships between persons the love goes both ways, with a complement of caring, emotional commitment, and trust. Just as this is true of friendship, it is true of romantic and marital love relationships. In fact in these cases the "relationship" is much more than a simple binary relationship, for which a subject and object of love are sufficient.[1] That love in a fully realized human love relationship, such as friendship or a romantic or marital relationship, is returned and has a richness that embraces emotions and behavior, does not negate the basic binary character of love, although it does highlight the latitude that is accommodated by that basic relationship.

The relational character of love may fairly easily be seen to apply in the familiar examples of trivial and profound love canvassed in the previous chapter and in evident variations. As one person may love another person, so of course one person may love several others, as when a parent loves her or his children. The basic subject-object pattern of love is still in evidence. It is only that the object has several members. The basic relational pattern of love

---

[1]   Mike Martin, whose main subject in *Love's Virtues* is "erotic" or romantic love between persons, argues that a range of virtues, including caring, faithfulness, and respect, provide a "structure" for romantic love.

also applies in less ordinary cases that may carry a suggestion of paradox. For instance, a child who has an imaginary friend may love that imaginary friend. It is not absolutely necessary that the object of love exists, although, as in this case, it may be psychologically necessary that the object is real to the one who loves it. Many continue to love those close to them who have died. After years of marriage, when one's partner in marriage dies, one may continue to love him or her. Even self-love fits this pattern. In self-love, though the subject and object are the same there are yet a subject and an object of love. The basic binary pattern of love is again present in the religious person's love of God, as it is in God's love for his people or his children or his creation, although in these cases, as in the case of friendship and marital love relationships, the full relationship is much beyond the simple subject-object binary relationship at its core.

At this point a further word or two on self-love and love for God are in order. Self-love of course can be thoroughly selfish. However, in the Christian tradition the self-love that is recognized is not a selfish self-love. Implicit in the command to "love your neighbor as yourself" (Mt. 22.39) is the idea of a proper self-love. Søren Kierkegaard (1813–55) in *Works of Love*, reflecting on the nature of proper self-love, says, "To love yourself in the right way and to love the neighbor correspond perfectly to one another; fundamentally they are one and the same thing."[2] For Kierkegaard such love disregards the difference between persons. One "blindly loves every human being" with "all dissimilarities . . . removed" and with no difference between "friend and enemy."[3] The idea of the love of others and of oneself without differentiation or distinction is also found in the writings and sermons of Meister Eckhart, who in a sermon said, "If you love yourself, you love all men as yourself. As long as you love one single person less than

---

2   Søren Kierkegaard, *Works of Love*, trans. and ed. Howard V. Hong and Edna H. Hong (Princeton, NJ: Princeton University Press, 1995), p. 22. *Works of Love* was originally published in 1847.

3   Kierkegaard, *Works of Love*, pp. 66, 67–68, and 69 (emphasis deleted).

yourself, you have never really loved yourself."[4] Simone Weil expresses the same idea when she says, "To love a stranger as oneself implies the reverse: to love oneself as a stranger."[5]

Central to several religious traditions is love of God, human love for God. This is so for the Western monotheisms, but also in other traditions, as in the Hindu *bhakti*, or devotional, tradition in which devotion and love are given to Vishnu, Shiva, or another god. In the Jewish and Christian traditions a primary commandment is to love God "with all your heart, and with all your soul" (Deut. 6.5 and Mt. 22.37). Yet love of God may seem to be conceptually paradoxical to some. How, many who do not believe in God might ask, can there be love for what does not exist? Without disputing the intuition behind the question that God does not exist, we can observe that the paradox of loving what does not exist is not distinctly religious and it is easily dispelled, for as our reflections have already revealed there are various examples of loving what does not exist, as when a child loves an imaginary friend. In quotidian examples most easily called to mind there is, to be sure, the *belief* that the one who is loved exists. A further religious paradoxicality relates to love for God in that, as will be argued in the next chapter, for an identifiable religious sensibility there can be love of God even when there is no belief in God.[6] For now, however, it is useful to see how explicit love of God is expressed by religious believers, for at least some of these expression are discernible by believers and nonbelievers alike. In its interior expressions believers' love of God may be hidden to view, but love of God may also be overtly expressed and discernible in many forms. For

---

4   Meister Eckhart, Sermon, trans. Frank Tobin, in *Meister Eckhart, Teacher and Preacher*, ed. Bernard McGinn (New York; Mahwah, NJ; and Toronto: Paulist Press, 1986), p. 268.

5   Simone Weil, *Gravity and Grace*, trans. Emma Crawford and Mario von der Ruhr (London and New York: Routledge, 1952), p. 62.

6   I will often refer to different religious sensibilities. By a religious sensibility I mean a religious orientation that a religious person may have that affects her or his beliefs, feelings, emotions, actions, and dispositions to act. A religious tradition can accommodate different religious sensibilities, and a religious person may have more than one.

instance, the Qur'an, which speaks of the love of God more than once, says of the religious that

> they feed, for the love
> Of God, the indigent,
> The orphan, and the captive. (76.8)[7]

One overt expression of the love of God in the three great monotheisms of the West is following God's commandments and teachings, as in giving to the poor and practicing charity. It is true that God's commandments can be followed out of fear, and when they are followed solely out of fear of God's retribution following them is not an expression of the love of God. Nevertheless, when "the law of his God is in his heart" (Ps. 38.31) and the believer follows God's law in his or her committed disposition, then following God's commandments may be an expression of his or her loving devotion to God.

Another expression of the love of God that may be overtly manifested is seen in many instances of thanking God. In the Christian tradition St. Paul says to give thanks to God "always and for everything" (Eph. 5.20). When God is loved all that is received and all that one sees about one are seen as manifestations of God's goodness. In many human love relationships the one loved is seen as good, as having goodwill at least toward oneself. So it is in the child-parent relationship and in mature friendships and marital relationships. Although love and trust are distinguishable, love in these cases involves trust as a part of itself. Love of God has this character as well, so that love of God and faith in God, with its trust, may be spoken of together. In this way love of God and trust in God tightly connect to God's goodness, although in contrast to human love relationships the goodness of God extends beyond oneself.

It extends to and suffuses all of God's creation. (In the book of Genesis [Gen. 1.31], all that God creates he beholds as very good.) This means that one expression of believers' love of God, which like obeying God's

---

7   All quotations from the Qur'an are from the translation by Abdullah Yusuf Ali.

commandments may be discernible even to nonbelievers, is that, though believers may be acutely aware of the grief and evil in the world, they do not see these as negating God's goodness. Some of those critical of religion, to be sure, have regarded the existence of moral evil (the evil or morally wrong things done by human beings) and natural evil (such as natural disasters, like earthquakes, and disease) as incompatible with God's existence.[8] However, no such incompatibility is countenanced by believers whose love and trust in God remain strong. With Job they will say, "the Lord gave and the Lord has taken away; blessed be the name of the Lord" (Job 1.21).

In another form religious love of God can be expressed in a yearning for God, as in Psalm 42, where the Psalmist longs for God as a hart longs for flowing streams.[9] In this form too the believer's devotion to God and love for God may be discernible to others in its exterior expressions. (We will return to love of God in chapter 6, and there consider certain questions and issues that arise for believers' love of God.)

III. IS LOVE AN EMOTIONAL PROCESS?

LOVE, unlike many instances of knowledge and belief, cannot exist with indifference toward its object. Love clearly has an affective or emotional dimension. Even in trivial cases of love, such as love for ice cream, there is an affect of pleasure or enjoyment that raises it above indifference. In love relationships between persons the affective dimension is inescapable in its prominence. This has led some to give a nearly exclusive importance to the emotional component of love and to discount love's relational nature.

Robert Solomon argues that love—or romantic love, which is his focus—is not a relationship. Love, he argues, is an "emotional process" that is an essentially

---

8   This position is centuries old. In modern times it was argued for by, for instance, J. L. Mackie and H. J. McCloskey. J. L Mackie, "Evil and Omnipotence" and H. J. McCloskey, "God and Evil," both reprinted in *God and Evil: Readings on the Theological Problem of Evil*, ed. Nelson Pike (Englewood Cliffs, NJ: Prentice-Hall, 1964).

9   The Psalmist by tradition is David (2 Sam. 23.1), even though many of the psalms have other authors.

private process of the "subjective self," even though one's love is directed to another. Relationships like marriage or a "dating pattern," for Solomon, are "social arrangements" with a "managerial" function. They help to regularize expectations and mutual obligations. Romantic love, however, he observes, may precede marriage or any such socially recognized relationship, even though a "fully developed love," Solomon allows, "requires the reciprocity of a relationship."[10]

Yet, love itself for Solomon is not a relationship. It is an emotional process interior to the lover. Love, he argues, can exist without the "social arrangement" of a relationship. This, he believes, is what occurs both when one continues to love another after his or her death and in the case of unrequited love.[11] Solomon is certainly right that love—romantic love in particular—can exist before and outside the public kinds of relationships that he considers, including marriage. But this does not mean that love is not itself a relationship. Yes, one can continue to love another after his or her death, but this does not show that love exists outside *all* relationships, for a love relationship can endure beyond death. Just as one honored and loved one's partner in life, one may honor and love her or him in death. We see something similar in making and keeping a promise. If one promises to look after another person's children after his or her death, one will violate that promise and the relationship it creates if one does not do so. Unrequited love, Solomon says, is "full-blown if not fully developed" love.[12] Here again he seems right. Unrequited love is love. Yet, though it is one-sided, it is still relational, not just in the sense that there is a core subject-object relationship, but in the further sense that unrequited love is unreturned love *for* a particular person, a particular man or woman from whom the lover longs for love in return. It is not free-floating, like free-floating anxiety, which has no particular object but attaches to everything.

Mike Martin observes that even if romantic love were an emotional process in which one redefines oneself, as Solomon suggests, that process

---

10   Robert C. Solomon, *About Love: Reinventing Romance for Our Times* (New York: Simon and Schuster, 1988), pp. 82–88.

11   Solomon, *About Love*, pp. 83–84.

12   Solomon, *About Love*, p. 85.

would have to occur in relation to the one who is loved.[13] Love, especially passionate romantic love, not only has an interior emotional dimension, but moreover there can be an emotional progression in love as a love relationship between two people develops and deepens. In this process there may be an increasing understanding of the other, a greater empathy and appreciation. Nevertheless, as Martin sees it, in romantic love this occurs within a relationship and is shaped by the particular relationship between particular persons. For this reason love cannot be identified with, and limited to, an interior process or "state of mind," as Solomon says. In addition love in its realization requires some kind of active interaction. In fully realized romantic love there is an interaction at several levels with the one who is loved, and here again we see the relational nature of love.

It is not at issue whether human love for another person, as in romantic love, or for other persons, as in family love, must have an emotional side. Love for God too must have an emotional or affective dimension. Otherwise love is jejune or empty, if it exists at all. In this respect love for another, like religious faith, is a passion that affects one's entire life, as Kierkegaard, who obliquely makes this point, was aware.[14] It affects the way we feel as well as the way we act. If Solomon meant only this much he would be right. This, however, does not make love in its romantic form, or in any of its forms, a "subjective" process, an interior soliloquy that just happens to take place with the thought of a particular person in mind.

IV. DOES LOVE BESTOW OR RECOGNIZE VALUE?

IN THE LAST SECTION the focus was on romantic love. In this section the focus will be on love between persons, the love one person gives to another, which includes romantic love but also, for instance, the love parents have for their

---

13   Martin, *Love's Virtues*, p. 189n38.

14   Søren Kierkegaard, *Fear and Trembling*, in *Fear and Trembling and Repetition*, trans. and ed. Howard V. Hong and Edna H. Hong (Princeton, NJ: Princeton University Press, 1983), pp. 122–23. *Fear and Trembling* was originally published in 1843.

children. In all cases of love between persons in giving love one responds to the other. And in some way value is involved. The value of the one loved, or the others who are loved, typically is felt, acknowledged, and insisted on by the one who loves. The expression of this sense of value may take several forms. Verbally it may be simply expressed by one's saying to the loved one or loved ones, "You are great!" or "You are the best!"

This much seems undeniable. However, there is a disagreement about the nature and the provenance of this value. Is it created by the love itself? Does love bestow value? Or is value recognized by the one who loves? Irving Singer in his discussion of the nature of love says, "[t]o love another person is to create a relationship in which that person takes on a new and sometimes irreplaceable value." As he sees it, love between persons, and romantic love in particular, consists of "appraisals" and "bestowals" of value, the bestowal of value being a "necessary condition" for love.[15] Both appraisals and bestowals, though, play a role in love, for Singer.

Appraisal is assessment of a prospective lover regarding his or her potential in satisfying one's needs, desires, and so on. Different properties of the prospective lover are assessed, such as intelligence and virility.[16] It is curious that Singer speaks of "appraisal" in relation to love, for appraisal or assessment seems more appropriate to making a purchase. We appraise different models of cars as we try to decide which to purchase, and we do so with our particular needs in mind. Singer perhaps uses the valuational term *appraisal*, rather than *recognition* of value, because he sees in love an approach to a prospective loved one in terms of a concern with one's own needs.

The bestowal of value on the one who is loved is very different from appraisal in Singer's treatment. When we bestow value we "create" value, he says.[17] It is bestowal of value that is more important for Singer. In fact, at one point he allows that "[a]ll appraisals must ultimately depend on bestowal since

---

15   Irving Singer, *The Modern World*, vol. 3 of *The Nature of Love* (Chicago: University of Chicago Press, 1987), p. 390.

16   Singer, *The Modern World*, p. 390.

17   Singer, *The Modern World*, p. 392. Singer italicizes *create* for emphasis.

[appraisals] presuppose that human beings give importance to the satisfaction of their needs and desires. Without such bestowal nothing could take on value of any sort."[18] If his category had been recognition his judgment might have been different.

The more basic issue is whether love bestows and so creates value or recognizes and so finds value in the one who is loved. A prima facie indication that value in the one loved is recognized is that in a love relationship, a person may come to regret not fully recognizing the value of the loved one earlier. Yet, apparently weighing on the other side, we sometimes see in others a wrongful imputation of value to the one that they love, and this may be seen as a misguided bestowal of value. It seems, however, that this could just as well be understood as a failure in recognition.

Alan Soble casts the underlying issue in his own way as an issue between what he calls "a-type" loves and "e-type" loves.[19] When love is a-type the one who loves finds "the properties" of the one who is loved to be valuable *because* he or she loves her or him. When love is e-type one loves another *because* one finds "the properties" of the other to be valuable. Like Singer, Soble focuses on the properties of the one loved or to be loved. Such properties might be intelligence or virility (which Singer mentions), but also a sturdy build, pretty eyes, politeness, or reliability, to name a few.

In a-type love, given Soble's category, love precedes the value that is given to the one loved. The source of value is a creation or *bestowal* (Soble uses the same term as Singer). For Soble a-type love is *agapeistic*, and he sees *agape* as involving bestowal, apparently because he is following Anders Nygren's characterization of *agape*. For Nygren *agape* is creative and imparts value.[20] As we will see, *agape* need not be understood in this way.

---

18   Singer, *The Modern World*, p. 393. Quoted by Alan Soble, *The Structure of Love* (New Haven and London: Yale University Press, 1990), p. 28.

19   Alan Soble, *The Philosophy of Sex and Love: An Introduction* (St. Paul, MN: Paragon House, 1998), p. 96. In his earlier *The Structure of Love* he used the same distinction but labeled the two types "agapic" and "erosic" love.

20   Anders Nygren, *Agape and Eros*, trans. Philip S. Watson (New York: Harper & Row, 1969), pp. 78 and 91. On p. 78, Nygren affirms the "value-creating" nature of Divine

In Soble's presentation e-type love, which for him is *eros*, by contrast finds value that exists before love. For Soble *philia*, the love of friendship, is a form of e-type love.[21] He does not mention *storge*, family love.

Soble and Singer do not agree on everything, but they agree that there is a significant place for bestowal of value in love between persons. For Singer bestowal is crucially present in all love between human beings; it complements appraisal, although appraisal itself is dependent on bestowal, he contends, as we noted. For Soble bestowal informs a-type or agapeistic love, but not e-type or *eros*-style love, which in Soble's typology recognizes value. Both authors thus provide answers to the question: Does love bestow or recognize value?

However, there is another way to address the question, and this other way rejects the bestowal-recognition dichotomy presupposed by the question when it is construed as a dichotomy between bestowing value on properties of the one loved and recognizing the value of properties of the one loved. For this other approach both *eros* and *agape* in regard to persons or God are best understood as *responses to persons or to God*. In *eros*, for this approach, there may be an awakening of love. The person one comes to love romantically may be someone not seen as particularly attractive for a period of time. Then there may be a sea change. One may "fall in love." Not all romantic love relationships are so dramatically entered of course. In some cultures marriages are arranged, and in these cases a love relationship may develop and deepen after marriage and over time, just as love may deepen in marriages that are not arranged. For *eros*, as exemplified by romantic love, there is certainly a response to the one who is loved and an appreciation of the one loved, but it is misguided to say *either* that the one who loves loves the other because of valuable properties she or he is found to have *or* that the one who loves gives value to the properties of the loved one because he or she loves him or her.

---

agape (God's love), and on p. 91, he says that the *agape* required of those who follow "the commandment of love," that is, the commandment to love God and to love your neighbor (Mt. 22. 37–39), "has its prototype in the Agape manifested by God" (emphasis deleted). *Agape and Eros* was originally published in Swedish in two volumes as *Eros and Agape*, 1930–36.

21   Soble, *The Philosophy of Sex and Love*, p. 96.

For *eros* in romantic love it is neither that one looks for some valuable property, finds it, and then begins to love, nor that love having begun remakes a property into a valuable property and then proceeds. In romantic love and other variants of love between persons that are forms of *eros*, the one who loves responds to the *person* who is loved. It is the loved person who is valued, although various properties of the person or persons who are loved may be praised and seen in the best light possible, and in this way both recognized in their value and given value.

Agape is altruistic love, given without any thought of return. Though it is anomalous to speak of "falling in love" in connection with *agape*, one may be moved to love *agapeistically* others one did not love before. One's heart is opened, we may say, using language that not accidentally has a religious resonance. For this approach, as it is exemplified in a distinct religious sensibility, in *agape* one finds others to be literally lovable—another person or several or all persons universally. They are responded to as they are, and as they are they are worthy of love. (In the Jewish and Christian traditions they have inherent worth in being in the image of God [Gen. 1.27].) It is not that there is love and then some property or properties of individuals are given value or that properties are seen to be valuable and then there is love. In *agapeistic* love, for this religious sensibility, one responds to others with love and appreciates the inherent worth or those loved, but that worth is not seen as created by their love or to be the preexisting reason upon the discovery of which their love follows.

V. IS LOVE RATIONAL?

FRANCIS BACON (1561–1626) in his essay *Of Love* observed, "It is impossible to love and be wise." Perhaps, though, it is possible for love to be rational or reasonable, or at least not at odds with reason. David Hume (1711–76) said that "reason is, and ought to be the slave of the passions."[22] What did he mean?

---

22   David Hume, *A Treatise of Human Nature*, ed. L. A. Selby-Bigge (Oxford: Clarendon Press, 1888), p. 415. Hume's *Treatise* was originally published 1739–40.

A passion for Hume is a motivating "impulse," a feeling that can move us to act, but has no "representative quality." For Hume all the passions—among which, in addition to love and hate, are hope, fear, and joy—have this character.[23] Reason, by contrast, as he saw it, though it could come to "judgments," could never move us to action. Passion decides our desired ends and moves us, while reason with its "representative" judgments decides the means to those ends. Thus reason is the "slave of the passions." Reason and passion, then, with their different functions, never meet on common ground. A passion could be called unreasonable in only two ways, Hume thought. First, if it is founded on the judgment of the existence of something and that thing does not exist (as in fear of the bogeyman); and second, when a passion moves us to action, we judge certain means sufficient to attain our desired end and they are not sufficient (as when we repeat an incantation to bring about hoped-for rain). In both instances, for Hume, it is really the "accompany[ing]" judgment that is unreasonable, not the passion itself. Love itself, as a passion, could never be "contrary to reason." Hume said, "'Tis not contrary to reason to prefer the destruction of the whole world to the scratching of my finger."[24] By extrapolation it is not contrary to reason to love money over one's family—or to love one's family over money. Love of anything is never unreasonable in being contrary to reason, but also it could never be reasonable by being in accord with reason. Hume's analysis is open to criticism, but if it is correct it both saves love in all its forms and regardless of its object from irrationality and excludes love from reasonableness.

Even without an appeal to Hume's analysis, it may seem to us that there are instances of love that are immune to a charge of irrationality. The question "Is your love for ice cream rational?" may elicit the reply, "I like ice cream!" And this seems to be a sufficient reply to whatever the question amounted to. Of course a different question, "Is it rational for you to eat so much ice cream?" might make good sense, especially when asked of someone with a health concern, such as diabetes. But this is not a question about one's love for ice cream per se.

---

23   Hume, *A Treatise of Human Nature*, pp. 415–16.

24   Hume, *A Treatise of Human Nature*, p. 416.

Love of ice cream, though, is a trivial form of love. Does the rationality question have a better purchase on more significant forms of love? It may well when rationality is construed as having a strong connection to self-interest. Rationality in one of its senses has such a connection; it was in this sense that eating too much ice cream might be irrational for one with diabetes. As it is treated in economic theory and often in philosophy rationality tends to be equated with self-interest as determined by one's self-interested desires, or, if a decision between courses of action is required, by a combination of the likelihood and the magnitude of the positive and negative consequences of the different actions as they affect one's self-interest. If this is the way rationality is understood then love for other persons, and especially *agape* as altruistic love, may necessarily be irrational, although some forms of transactional love may qualify as rational.

Transactional love is a type of love, in one classification of types that was identified in the previous chapter. It is love given with the thought and expectation of reciprocation. In this form of love there is an explicit or implicit agreement as to what each in the love relationship gives and gets. The agreement might even be negotiated. If its terms are in the self-interest of those in the relationship, then in this view of rationality the love is rational. If the terms favor the self-interest of only one of those in the relationship, then that person's love is rational, although the love given in return by his or her partner is not.

Some might object that transactional love does not seem to be love. However, if we can include under the broad polythetic umbrella of love selfish as well as unselfish love, as it seems we can, then transactional love should also be recognized, even though it may be very far from *agapeistic* love or the love Simone Weil had in mind when she said, "To love the soul of a woman is not to think of her as serving one's own pleasure, etc."[25]

There are other ways to think about what is rational or reasonable. Another way that is found in much of our common discourse grounds the

---

25   Simone Weil, *Gravity and Grace*, trans. Emma Crawford and Mario von der Ruhr (London and New York: Routledge, 1952), p. 66.

rational or reasonable in appropriateness. Reasonable attire for a wedding guest is appropriate attire. A reasonable highway speed is one that is appropriate given the driving conditions. We will return to this understanding of reasonableness as appropriateness and its application to love later, but not until chapter 10.

VI. LOVE AND DENIAL OF SELF

LOVE CAN BE SELFISH OR UNSELFISH. The love of money or power, sought for personal satisfaction, may forthrightly be confessed to be selfish. Despite an initial impression that it is an oxymoron, selfish love of another person is also possible, as when the lover's primary concern is his own pleasure. These selfish forms of love and the forms of love that are a matter of personal taste and preference, such as love for sports or travel, are not viable candidates for self-denial. Other forms of love for another or others, especially *agapeistic* forms, are more promising candidates for love with self-denial.

In a realized love relationship in which love is given and received, one person or both may love selfishly. But in some relationships in which love is fully realized, love may be given with no thought of benefit to oneself. In these cases love is *agape*, or like *agape*, and in these cases there can be self-denial in love.

Yet, as selfish love of another person may at first seem conceptually odd, so might it seem strained to speak of *agape* in romantic love. Can there be *agape* in a romantic and sensual love relationship? It is important to appreciate that the antithesis of *agape* is not *eros*. *Agape* is altruistic love, and its antithesis is not *eros* but love given for the sake of love in return, or for the sake of pleasure, as in transactional love. The antithesis of *eros* is lassitudinous and dispassionate love, not *agape*. *Agape* does not rule out *eros*, and *eros* does not rule out *agape*. A yearning love for another or for God that is love with no thought of return is both *agape* and *eros*.

Both *agape* and *eros* in their individual natures may be strongly expressed. *Eros* is often if not always overtly passionate in its expression, and this is particularly true of *eros* in its romantic and erotic form. But this is also true of *eros* in its religious form, in which it is an intense longing for God. In both forms there may be a strong, nearly visceral yearning. However, both *eros* and *agape* are passions. Not both are passions in Hume's sense of "impulse" or feeling, but both are passions in Kierkegaard's sense of passion, in that each can claim and direct one's entire life. *Eros* and *agape*, then, are not opposed because one is a passion and the other is not. When *eros* is identified with erotic or sensual love, it may be thought to be opposed to *agape* because erotic or sensual love is often seen as self-concerned with one's own pleasure. And often it may be, but it need not be. Here we should recall Joseph Runzo's concept of "seraphic love," in which *agape* and *eros* are united.

In fact in some religious discussions of *agape* and *eros* the relationship between them is even closer. Simon Tugwell observes that Pseudo-Dionysius "refuted on philological grounds the distinction that evidently some people were making . . . between *eros* and *agape*."[26] Dionysius, or Pseudo-Dionysius, observed in *The Divine Names*, that in the scriptures we will find it said about the divine wisdom, "I yearned for her beauty," and he says, "let us not fear this title of 'yearning' [*eros*] nor be upset by what anyone has to say about these two names, for, in my opinion, the sacred writers regard 'yearning' [*eros*] and 'love' [*agape*] as having one and the same meaning."[27] Dionysius is referring to the Wisdom of Solomon 8.2. The full verse from which he quotes is in one translation.

> She [wisdom] it was I [Solomon] loved and searched for from
>   my youth,
> I resolved to have her for my bride,
> I fell in love with her beauty.

---

26   Simon Tugwell, O.P., *Ways of Imperfection: An Exploration of Christian Spirituality* (Springfield, IL: Template Publishers, 1985), p. 162.

27   Dionysius, *The Divine Names*, chap. 4, 12, 709B, in *Pseudo-Dionysius: The Complete Works*, trans. Colm Luibheid (New York and Mahwah, NJ: Paulist Press, 1987), p. 81. In accord with a received practice of his day that allowed writing under the name of an illustrious predecessor, the fifth- or sixth-century author of *The Divine Names* presented himself as Dionysius the Areopagite, the contemporary of St. Paul (Acts 17.34).

He also refers to Proverbs 4.6 and 8, which in the translation he quotes is

> Yearn for her and she shall keep you;
>
> exalt her and she will extol you;
>
> honor her and she will embrace you.

Dionysius as well speaks of "the yearning of God."[28]

If Dionysius is right, *agape* and *eros* are one and the same. If Runzo is right, though, they are different, they are compatible and can be united. If either is right, *agape* and *eros* are not opposed, in accord with our argument. Arguably, then, in romantic love and in religious *eros* or yearning love, or along with them, there could also be the self-denial that *agape* allows and requires.

❦ THE LOVE that the asymptote of love approaches is love at its highest, uttermost love. The love that approaches uttermost love as love is relational. It could not be conceived as a subjective emotional process, although it may have—must have—an essential affective dimension. It should not be conceived of as bestowing or creating value in what is loved. It will respond to what is loved. What will uttermost love or a religious love that begins to approach it love? Will it be rational or reasonable, and if so how so? Will it embody denial of self, and if so how so? What will be the "works" of uttermost love? And how will it be expressed? These questions have yet to be addressed.

---

28   Dionysius, *The Divine Names*, chap 4, sections 11, and 12, 709A and 709B, in *Pseudo-Dionysius: The Complete Works*, pp. 80–81, and nn.152 and 154.

Chapter Three

Love of Others

I. INTRODUCTION

IN THE WORLD OF HUMAN AFFAIRS the most serious and most prevalent form of love is love of others. Very few people in the cultures of the world are untouched by some form of love between persons: the love parents give to their children, children to parents, spouses to one another, family love, the love of friendship. Often that love, or its absence, will have a life-significance for those who give it and those who return it. A less intimate form of love between persons is the wider love for one's fellow human beings—less intimate but real enough when it is expressed in our response to the needs of others half a world away who are afflicted by famine or the disasters of nature.

All the major religions of the world in some way recognize the love or compassion that is to be given to others within and beyond our ken. In the Torah and in the New Testament there is the commandment to "love your neighbor as yourself" (Lev. 19.18 and Mt. 22.39), just as in each there is the commandment to love God with all your heart and all your soul. In the Jewish and Christian traditions God's unfailing love is the model or ideal of the love to be given to the neighbor. Religious love of neighbor in these traditions is a part of the love that begins to approach the endpoint of the asymptote of love, conceived of as God's love.

Love of neighbor in the Jewish and Christian traditions, like compassion in the Buddhist tradition, and love of others or benevolence in other traditions, is importantly manifested in exterior action but also in one's interior action and disposition. It has an essential affective dimension. It is in biblical language expressed through the disposition of our hearts (Deut. 15.7). Beyond this, though, there is some question about how love for others, taking God's love as its ideal, is to be expressed.

In section II we will begin to explore the religious understanding of love of others, as found in the Christian tradition, by drawing on the Christian parable of the Good Samaritan.

At times a religious understanding of the requirements of love can seem to be at odds with ethical requirements, as perhaps sometimes they are. In section III we will reflect on the tensions between religious and ethical requirements.

Section IV will bring us to the questions: Can one love God *through* loving others? and Can one love others without loving God? In a plethora of cases it would seem indisputably possible to love others without loving God. But this question relates to love of others that is love of neighbor. Even so, it seems that one can love others without loving God. Contrary to what may seem evident, it will be seen that for an identifiable religious sensibility we cannot love others as our neighbors without loving God.

II. THE UNDUE DEMANDS OF LOVE OF NEIGHBOR

IN THE NEW TESTAMENT when Jesus confirms that the second great commandment is to love your neighbor as yourself, he is asked, "And who is my neighbor?" (Lk.10. 27–29). Jesus replies with the parable of the Good Samaritan. In the parable Jesus does not directly address the question he was asked but instead shows what it is to love a neighbor. In Jesus' parable a man has been robbed and beaten and left half-dead by the side of the road. One following the other, two worthy men of the community come along the road. Each seeing the man there in his sorry state crosses to the other side of the road and passes him by. The third man to come by, a Samaritan, has compassion and gives him aid. He binds up his wounds and takes him to an inn, where he cares for him and pays the innkeeper to continue caring for him in his absence. "Which of these three ... proved neighbor to the man who fell among the robbers?" Jesus asks. The answer he wants, expects—and gets— from his hearer is clear. "Go and do likewise," Jesus then says (Lk. 10.30–37).

Jesus does not directly answer the question "Who is my neighbor?" Yet in showing what it is to be a loving neighbor to another who is in need (and whom others have passed by) he indirectly answers the question. Samaritans in Jesus' time were considered inferior by many mainstream Jews. Jesus does not enunciate the lesson that even the Samaritan is your neighbor. His lesson is more subtly and effectively taught. Jesus brings the one to whom he tells the parable to see that even the person in dire need he may want to disregard is his neighbor, and that the Samaritan has been a neighbor in response to his need.

In this way Jesus addresses the more important question of what it is to be a neighbor. Jesus says, "Go and do likewise." In the parable the Samaritan acts from compassion. A part of "doing likewise," then, is to respond from the disposition of one's heart, freely with spontaneity and alacrity, to the needs of others. This goes beyond conventional ethical understanding, according to which we should care for our own, grudgingly or otherwise, and care for strangers in need only when it is convenient and without risk.[1] No doubt the first two men in the parable who encountered the man who was set on by robbers did not think that they were required to stop and give aid, and as far as conventional ethics go they may have been right.

The commandment to love your neighbor is to love your neighbor *as yourself*. Love of oneself is not forbidden. It even is a part of the commandment or implicit in it. In the previous chapter we discussed the character of the love that one is to have for oneself. It is love given without distinction between oneself and the next person or between other persons. It accords completely with the Golden Rule, which Jesus teaches with the words "as you wish that men do to you, do so to them" (Lk. 6.31).

Love without differentiation between oneself and others, we should be clear, is not the same as love without difference in the expression of love. Love of neighbor embraces love of one's spouse and of one's children, but the loving

---

1   It is assumed that these conventional moral expectations prevailed in the first century as they prevail today. Evidence for this is that it is such morally accepted expectations that give the parable of the Good Samaritan, and other biblical passages, such as Lev. 19.18 and 34, their point.

support given to one's husband or wife will be different from the nurturing love given to young children. Moreover the spousal love that is supportive and required in one marital relationship may be very different from the spousal love required in another marital relationship, as the nurturing love given to different children may be different. This applies as well to the love of neighbor in its broader scope. The loving care given to the man set upon by robbers, which answers his needs, will be different from the expression of love given to others with other needs.

Love of neighbor is *agape*, which allows, as we saw in the previous chapter, that it might also be *eros*, as when it is love of one's beloved or love of God. God's love for human beings is *agape* at its zenith, in its highest and infinite expression. Human *agape* for others would have God's love, the endpoint of the asymptote of human *agape*, as an ideal. For Anders Nygren God's *agape* bestows or creates value. It does not respond to the value of those who are loved, since, as Nygren holds, "the man who is loved by God has no value in himself."[2] Human *agape* for one's neighbors has a similar nature, for Nygren. It is difficult, however, to say that human *agape* for God bestows value on God.[3] The better view of *agape* in the three forms before us—God's love for human beings, human love for God, and human love for one's neighbors—is that it is a responsive love, responding to human persons and their inherent value or to God, which keeps in place a unified nature for *agape* as love.

III. "HATE HIS OWN FATHER AND MOTHER"

THE DEMANDS OF RELIGIOUS LOVE for one's neighbors are undue in relation to the requirements of conventional morality, for they take us beyond our ordinary ethical reactions and thinking. Also they may be more seriously

---

2   Anders Nygren, *Agape and Eros*, trans. Philip S. Watson (New York: Harper & Row, 1969), p. 78.

3   Alan Soble makes essentially this observation about Nygren's understanding of *agape* and goes on to discuss Nygren's effort to construe human love for God in terms of faith. Soble, *The Structure of Love*, p. 21. He cites p. 127 of Nygren's *Agape and Eros*, where Nygren explicitly says, "Faith is love towards God."

opposed to our accustomed morality in being antithetical to our ordinary ethical thinking. So it is with the "hard saying" in Luke:

> If anyone comes to me and does not hate his own father and mother
> and wife and children and brothers and sisters, yes, and even his own
> life, he cannot be my disciple. (Lk. 14.26)

Jesus' words are about discipleship, and he is saying that loyalty in discipleship will require a turning from concern for family and self-concern.[4] But if we allow that members of our family are among our neighbors, Jesus' words also relate to religious love. Religious love for family, it appears, requires hate. It seems, then, that if we allow that ordinary morality requires us not to hate our father, mother, and children, the demands of religious love conflict with the demands of morality. How are we to understand this conflict?

Morality, or the ethical, has been understood in several different ways.[5] For instance, within theoretical reflection in the Western philosophical tradition two of the main approaches to understanding morality are the Kantian, which regards moral duties or obligations as existing independently of the effects of human actions, and the utilitarian, or more broadly the consequentialist approach, which regards obligation and moral rightness as determined by the good and bad effects of human actions. However, the thinking of both Kantians and consequentialists, as well as that of other philosophical approaches to understanding morality, is theoretical reflection on the pretheoretical phenomenon of morality, and the morality that contrasts with religion is just that pretheoretical morality. In our discussion of the parable of the Good Samaritan, we contrasted the loving care provided by the Samaritan

---

4   Rick F. Talbott discusses this aspect of Jesus' teaching in his *Jesus, Paul, and Power* (Eugene, OR: Cascade Books, 2010), pp. 49–57.

5   Sometimes a distinction is drawn between ethics and morality. Often the former is taken to be more reflective on principles, the latter more a matter of behavior, although a difference between ethics and morality is sometimes otherwise stipulated. In ordinary parlance, though, the two terms are used more or less interchangeably; and even in critical reflection they tend to merge, so that in philosophical ethics one may speak of either "moral relativism" or "ethical relativity" in addressing the issue of relativism.

with the requirements of conventional morality. Morality we understood as conventional morality, the pretheoretical de facto morality that in some form is recognized by all or nearly all human beings. With this meaning in place the question can be raised: How do the demands of morality, or ethical demands, relate to religious demands?

One answer is that pretheoretical morality in its highest development coincides with religious demands. Setting aside the complication that religious demands may vary from one religion to another in certain particulars and allowing that the *main* requirements of the major religions regarding human behavior greatly coincide, we may allow that this answer is essentially correct. All the major religions of the world, it has been observed, recognize in some way the Golden Rule.[6] However this answer contemplates morality in its ideal development, not as the conventional morality most live by.

Another answer is that religion is more demanding than morality, or differently demanding. This is the answer we are driven to when we take morality to be conventional morality, as we were driven to it in considering the parable of the Good Samaritan.

Søren Kierkegaard in *Fear and Trembling* was concerned with the demands of religion in their opposition to the demands of the ethical. His effort in *Fear and Trembling*, as elsewhere, was to bring into relief the demands of faith, but in *Fear and Trembling* he, or his pseudonymous voice Johannes de Silentio, also treats the difference between religious and ethical demands. For Kierkegaard in *Fear and Trembling*, faith requires religious, not ethical, commitment. Kierkegaard's strategy in *Fear and Trembling* is to retell the story of Abraham, the exemplar of faith, whose faith is tested by God. The background story that Kierkegaard draws on is in the book of Genesis (Gen. 12, 17, and 22).

---

6   John Hick, *An Interpretation of Religion: Human Responses to the Transcendent*, 2nd ed. (New Haven and London: Yale University Press, 2004), p. 313. That the various religions are similar in their primary behavioral requirements is widely recognized. For instance, the Dalai Lama says in reference to "the world's major religions" that each "promotes the same basic values" and "stress ... cultivating love and compassion." His Holiness the Dalai Lama, *Ethics for the New Millennium* (New York: Riverhead Books, 1999), pp. 20 and 123.

It is not unimportant to Kierkegaard that this is a biblical story. Yet, strictly, Kierkegaard could have used it even if it were not part of the canon but only a religious story that in its narrative contains the demands of faith.

In the book of Genesis Abraham is called on by God to leave "his country" and go to a new land (Gen. 12.1). This Abraham does, though he is seventy-five years old. When Abraham is ninety-nine, God promises him that he will be "the father of a multitude of nations" (Gen. 17.4). His wife Sarah will in her old age bear him a son to be named Isaac, and through him and his descendants God's promise will be realized (Gen. 17.19). But then God tests Abraham. God commands Abraham to take Isaac to the land of Moriah and there to present him as a burnt offering (Gen. 22.2). This test of Abraham's faith is recognized in both the Christian tradition and the Jewish tradition, in which it is the "binding" or *Akedah*. It is also recognized in the Islamic tradition. In the Qur'an, the story of Abraham's trial of faith is recounted (37.101–9), but Abraham's son is not named and in the Islamic tradition he is understood to be Ishmael.

Kierkegaard in his retelling of Abraham's trial of faith emphasizes what he sees as essential elements of Abraham's faith, all of which are compatible with Genesis, though they are implicit in the biblical story. For Kierkegaard Abraham must not doubt that Isaac will live in order for his faith to be whole.[7] He must be certain that Isaac will live even if he goes through with the sacrifice. And he is certain. He knows that Isaac will live, for God has promised him that through Isaac he will be the "father of nations." He is to be the father of faith and the father of nations of the faithful. His faith is in God, trust in God that God will keep his promise, and that trust comes to a crucial focus in Abraham's not doubting that Isaac will live even if he is called on to complete the sacrifice.

For Kierkegaard, then, Abraham does not think that he will kill Isaac. He believes, and has no doubt, that Isaac will live. Still, for Kierkegaard, Abraham is not within the ethical. There is, he says, a "teleological suspension of the

---

7   Søren Kierkegaard, *Fear and Trembling*, in *Fear and Trembling and Repetition*, trans. and ed. Howard V. Hong and Edna H. Hong (Princeton, NJ: Princeton University Press, 1983), pp. 20–35.

ethical" in the story of Abraham.[8] In order to understand what Kierkegaard means by a "teleological suspension of the ethical" we need to appreciate how in *Fear and Trembling* he understood "the ethical." It is "the universal" in two senses. First, it applies in all its demands universally, to each and all. Second, it is "disclosed" universally. It is understandable to each and all in its demands.[9] It is, then, essentially the conventional morality that all understand and follow. Abraham departs from the ethical in that his action—preparing his son for sacrifice—is *not* ethical. It is not because it does not meet the second condition. What he is doing is not understandable universally. It is not understandable to his ethical neighbors. In an ethical or conventional moral understanding one does not prepare one's son as a sacrifice. Ethically the expression for what he is doing is that he means to murder his son, for this is what common ethical sense sees.[10] Abraham does not mean to kill his son. He knows beyond doubt that Isaac will live. But to his neighbors Abraham is a madman. If Abraham is to keep his "absolute duty" to God he must depart from the ethical and there must be a suspension of the ethical, which indeed there is in Kierkegaard's account.

Kierkegaard's understanding applies to Luke 14.26, and Kierkegaard himself makes the connection.[11] Ethically Abraham hates Isaac, for his action ethically understood is an expression of hate. It is *literally* hate, for its literal meaning is a matter of what is universally understood.[12] But if he "actually hates Isaac, he can rest assured that God does not demand this of him.... He must love Isaac with his whole soul."[13] So ethically he hates Isaac, but religiously in relation to his absolute duty to God he must and does love Isaac. Isaac is to him most dear and Abraham knows that, though he follows God's

---

8   Kierkegaard, *Fear and Trembling*, p. 66.

9   Kierkegaard, *Fear and Trembling*, pp. 54 and 82.

10   Kierkegaard, *Fear and Trembling*, p. 30.

11   Kierkegaard, *Fear and Trembling*, p. 72.

12   Kierkegaard, *Fear and Trembling*, p. 73.

13   Kierkegaard, *Fear and Trembling*, p. 74.

command, not only will he not lose Isaac but he will give to Isaac the most precious gift of all, the gift of faith. Applied to Luke 14.26 Kierkegaard's lesson is that ethically, and literally—in the eyes of conventional morality—we are called on to hate our father and mother, but we fail to understand and follow the commandment if we actually hate our father and mother.

Here we may want to ask, How does the distinction between *literally hate* and *actually hate* apply to those named in Luke 14.26, one's father, mother, wife (or husband), brothers, sisters, and oneself? Kierkegaard makes it clear enough how Abraham ethically and literally hates Isaac while actually loving Isaac, but he does not give the distinction a concrete instantiation in relation to Luke 14.26. And we should recognize that while Luke 14.26 names in addition to oneself only family members, its import also applies to national and community allegiances, and to ethnic, clan, and caste relationships.

If we keep in mind the sense of the ethical as conventional ethical thinking or conventional morality, which is about what Kierkegaard means by the ethical, something more can be said. Conventional ethical treatment may allow bias and favorable treatment. A merchant acts ethically in terms of conventional morality if he or she charges his or her special customers less and strangers more. A judge will have conventional moral approval if he or she gives a more lenient sentence to those toward whom the community is partial. Family and caste favoritism may even be seen as a moral duty. In these cases if bias, partiality, and special treatment are not followed, those who would have been favored are in the terms of conventional morality being hated.

The loving care given by the Samaritan to the man set upon by robbers answers his needs. Love of one's neighbors will respond to the needs of strangers. Such a response to the needs of strangers, within limits, may be allowed by conventional morality as long as it does not materially impinge on meeting the desires of those close to one—one's father and mother and other family relations named in Luke 14.26, and by extension others with whom one feels a close association. If it does then ethically this again amounts to hate. Ethically there are limits to the love that may be given to strangers.

The passage in Luke ends with saying that one must hate "even [one's own] life." But just as actually loving one's father, mother, spouse, children, and brothers and sisters is not ruled out by religious love, so loving oneself rightly is not ruled out. Religiously, as opposed to ethically, love is given without limits, but religious love is not given out of self-concern.[14] Ethically one may be *very* concerned about oneself, and not acceding to one's various desires in a measured way will, in many cases, ethically register as hatred of oneself.

IV. CAN ONE LOVE GOD THROUGH LOVING OTHERS? AND CAN ONE LOVE OTHERS WITHOUT LOVING GOD?

IN THE TORAH and in the New Testament there is the commandment to love God and there is the commandment to love your neighbor. In the New Testament these are the two great commandments (Mt. 22. 36–39). Also in the New Testament, in John's first letter, the possibility of one's loving God without loving one's "brother" is vigorously denied: "If anyone says, 'I love God,' and hates his brother, he is a liar" (1 Jn. 4.20).[15] It is another question, though, whether one can love God through loving others, and yet another whether one can love others, one's neighbors, without loving God. These are the questions before us.

For some forms of the love of others it may be obvious that one can love others without loving God. The man who selfishly loves a woman for his own pleasure may not have love for God. But our question relates to the love of neighbor, love for one's brothers and sisters. Can one have that love without loving God? Miguel de Unamuno in his short story "Saint Manuel Bueno, Martyr" presents a life—that of Don Manuel, a parish priest in a small Spanish village—that is relevant to this question.

Don Manuel is quietly effective as a priest. He says mass for the people of Valverde de Lucerna and hears their confessions. More than this he is deeply engaged with the trials and tribulations of the people of the village. He saves marriages, reconciles parents and children, and consoles those who have

---

14　Arguably, neither proper self-love nor self-respect is ruled out by religious love. For a discussion of the relation of self-concern to self-love and self-respect, see chapter 11 of *Dying to Self and Detachment* (Farnham, UK and Burlington, VT: Ashgate, 2012).

15　In Kierkegaard's terms what is meant is *actually* hates, as opposed to *ethically* hates.

become bitter. His presence and gaze are such that he seems to effect miraculous cures. He loves the people of Valverde de Lucerna and shows his wisdom in the sensitivity of his support. For instance, when a girl of the village who had gone to the city returns with an illegitimate son, Don Manuel prevails on the man in the village who had loved her and whom she had left for the city to marry her and give her son his name. Years later the man becomes an invalid, and the boy is his consolation. Don Manuel is the opposite of remote or contemplative. He often engages in village activities in ways other priests would be reluctant to do, as when he plays the drum at the village dance for young people. In all his activities and interchanges his near-saintliness is evident, and his inspiration and support are felt by all in the village.

However, Don Manuel has a secret that he keeps from the village. As he says the Nicene Creed in unison with the congregation, when they get to the last verse about life everlasting he falls silent, although his silence is generally undetected. Unamuno is not altogether clear about the full extent of Don Manuel's doubt, but it does not violate the narrative of the story that Don Manuel does not believe in God.

Unamuno's narrator, Angela, who like everyone else in the village is devoted to Don Manuel, tells how Don Manuel converted her brother Lazarus to the faith. When Lazarus returns from America with some saved money, he is dubious about both village life and the faith. Don Manuel and he start taking walks together, and Lazarus gains a sense of the priest's dedication to the people of Valverde de Lucerna. Don Manuel does not inculcate the catechism, about which he himself has doubts, but by his example he converts Lazarus to his own way of being religious. Lazarus, who becomes Don Manuel's friend and disciple, comes to understand his secret, but he also understands that Don Manuel with his ability to console and support those in the village in their belief is protecting them from the torments of the doubt that he himself endures.[16]

---

16   Miguel de Unamuno, "Saint Manuel Bueno, Martyr," trans. Anthony Kerrigan, in *Great Spanish Stories*, ed. Angel Flores (New York: Modern Library, 1956), pp. 336–79, esp. 339, 340, 342, 345, 357, and 359.

Angela, who is a devout Catholic, toward the end of the story she is telling confesses that she is

> of the opinion that Don Manuel the Good, my Don Manuel, and my brother, too, died believing they did not believe, but that, without believing in their belief, they actually believed.[17]

If Angela and Unamuno are right, Don Manuel believed without believing that he believed. Our question is not whether one can believe in God without believing that he or she believes, but whether one can love one's sisters and brothers without loving God. This question too relates to Don Manuel, but not to him alone. Say that one is an avowed atheist, unlike Don Manuel who in spite of his doubts may have believed unconsciously if Unamuno is right. Such an unbeliever could yet love men and women universally in an active and self-sacrificing manner, but would she or he have love for God? Or say that one believes in God, or at least that God exists, but rejects God, as Ivan Karamazov in Dostoyevsky's *The Brothers Karamazov* rejected God, without denying God's existence. Could such a rejecter of God yet love God? Say that one loves one's neighbors universally in a self-sacrificing way. Would this person also love God?

It is easy and seemingly quite logical to reason that to love God one must believe that God exists, and to reason that to love God one must not reject God. But religiously and spiritually matters may be more subtle. Religiously one's heart may be turned to God, while one's intellect rejects God or denies his existence. Read one way this is an implicit lesson of the parable of the King (Mt. 25.31–40). The parable relates to the Last Judgment and who will be chosen and not chosen to inherit the kingdom. However, it also has implications for the love of God. The king says to those "blessed of my Father" that

> I was hungry and you gave me food, I was thirsty and you gave me drink, I was a stranger and you welcomed me, I was naked and you clothed me, I was sick and you visited me, I was in prison and you came to me.

---

17   Unamuno, "Saint Manuel Bueno, Martyr," p. 375.

The righteous ask him, "Lord, when did we see thee hungry and feed thee? And when did we see thee a stranger and welcome thee, or naked and clothe thee [or] sick or in prison and visit thee?" The king answers, "as you did it to the least of these my brethren, you did it to me." In loving "the least of these my brethren," the righteous have loved God.

Of course this is not the only reading of the parable, but it is a reading that accords with a viable religious sensibility. On this reading, Don Manuel and others who love their neighbors as themselves implicitly love God, even with no thought of God. Simone Weil says that it is a method of purification "to pray to God not only in secret as far as men are concerned, but with the thought that God does not exist," and "If we love God while thinking that he does not exist, he will manifest his existence."[18] Simone Weil's mystical perception, which contradicts the seemingly logical principle that to love a being one must believe that that being exists, is closer to the reality of loving God in the strain of religious understanding and sensibility we have drawn on in the above reflections.

In that strain of religious sensibility one implicitly loves God *through* loving one's fellow human beings. Can one love one's neighbors without loving God? If we answer that one can, then we will think that it is possible to love one's fellow humans with dedication and selfless action while *not* loving God; and we will think that there can be no love of God when God is not believed to exist. The contrasting answer given by the religious sensibility we have drawn on is that we cannot fail to love God if our love is not selfish and truly directed to others. Our love of others becomes love of God as well. When Simone Weill says that "supernatural love touches only creatures and goes only to God," her thought is again close to this religious sensibility.[19] This religious sensibility, in affirming that there is no love of others without love of God, is not saying that we must fail to love others if we have no thought of God, it is saying, rather, that, even with no thought of God, if we love others in the right way

---

18   Simone Weil, *Gravity and Grace*, trans. Emma Crawford and Mario von der Ruhr (London and New York: Routledge, 1952), pp. 15 and 20.

19   Simone Weil, *Gravity and Grace*, p. 62.

we will thereby implicitly love God. Love of God cannot be escaped by those who truly love their neighbors. This religious sensibility emphasizes the paramount importance of the alignment of one's heart in religious love. Even if one's intellect denies that there is a God, or rejects God, if from one's heart one loves one's neighbors, one's love reaches to God as well. So this religious sensibility understands the parable of the King.

Chapter Four

Knowledge of God and Love of God

I. INTRODUCTION

FROM THE PERSPECTIVE of the religious sensibility we discussed in the previous chapter, and given its understanding of love for God, human beings can love God even with no thought of God through their dedicated love of others. Such love of God is *implicit* love, in contrast to an *explicit* love of God consciously directed to God. Many who recognize the possibility and validity of implicit love for God also acknowledge that explicit love of God is closer to a fully realized love of God.

The two great commandments of Christianity are commandments to love, and love in the Christian tradition is recognized as the paramount virtue (1 Cor. 13.13). Also important in the Western Abrahamic traditions is knowledge of God and of his commandments, although, especially in the Christian tradition, there is a certain ambivalence about knowledge. St. Paul writes to the Corinthians that "'Knowledge puffs up, but love builds up" (1 Cor. 8.1). Paul is referring to the specific knowledge that what is offered to idols may be eaten without violating Christian precepts, although, he says, one's doing so may prove a "stumbling block to the weak" (1 Cor. 8.9). Paul's focus here, then, is on specific knowledge, which is perhaps held pridefully and exercised without proper attention to the susceptibility of others. It does not "build up" as love does. The "love of Christ," Paul says, "surpasses knowledge" (Eph. 3.19). But also Paul writes to the Corinthians, "among the mature we do impart wisdom ... a secret and hidden wisdom of God" (1 Cor. 2.6–7), and his prayer for the Ephesians is that they may be given "a spirit of wisdom and reve-lation in the knowledge of him [Christ]" (Eph. 1.17), as his prayer for the Philippians is that "your love may abound more and more with knowledge and all discernment" (Phil. 1.9). Knowledge of God is not unequivocally ruled out in the New Testament. Jesus says, "I am the good shepherd. I know my own and they know me, as the Father knows me and I know the Father" (Jn. 10. 14–15).

The kind of religious knowledge that Paul approvingly refers to is knowledge that is *given* or *revealed* to believers. In the theological tradition of the Middle Ages another source of knowledge of God was recognized: natural reason. Within the early and developing Christian tradition, then, there undeniably was, and is, some place for religious knowledge, including knowledge of God. Two questions that arise at this point are: What is the nature of this knowledge of God? and What is its relation to love of God?

In the section II we will look at what might be called theological knowledge of God and why it has seemed to many that such knowledge would not nec-essarily quicken love for God.

Then in section III we will examine the thesis that to know God *is* to love God. If this thesis is correct in its strong form there is no knowing God without loving God.

In section IV we will turn to knowledge of God and of God's love that is experiential, as opposed to intellectual.

II. WHY IT SEEMS THAT ONE CAN KNOW GOD AND NOT LOVE GOD

THERE IS A DISTINCTION between knowing *what* God is and knowing *that* God is. Both what God is (God's nature) and that God is (God's existence) are religiously important in the theistic traditions and felt to be important by many believers. Both have been matters of theological concern. The issue of whether one can know God and not love God relates to both knowing what God is and knowing that God is. Accordingly we will divide the issue and consider these two aspects of knowledge of God in order.

Knowing What God Is

St. Anselm (1033–1109), who became the Archbishop of Canterbury in 1093, allowed in the *Proslogion* that even those who say that God does not exist understand what God is. God is by his nature, for Anselm "something than which nothing greater can be thought." That is, God is the Supreme Being (than which nothing greater can even be thought).[1] The idea of God as the Supreme Being, which is in accord with the modern dictionary definition of "God," is both familiar and intuitive to believers and nonbelievers alike. Anselm is simply using the received pretheological idea or concept of God. Even one who denies that God exists understands that this is what God is, Anselm observed; even he, or she, has the idea of God in his or her understanding or mind, as Anselm puts it; but, Anselm said, "he does not understand that it [God] exists."[2] Anselm clearly recognized, then, that one can have the true concept of God, know what God is, and not believe that God exists. This means furthermore, although Anselm does not say so, that he allowed one who does not believe God exists, but knows what God is, would not respond to God with *explicit* love, for such a person would deny that there is a God to respond to.

Since Anselm's time, and particularly in today's world, it has been widely recognized that atheists and agnostics know what God is—the Supreme Being possessing the perfections. They may even be able to fill out the concept more fully drawing on one or more religious traditions. But they deny or doubt that such a being exists. While, given the argument of the previous chapter, they might implicitly love God, they would not explicitly love God.

---

1   St. Anselm, *Proslogion*, chap. II, in *St. Anselm's Proslogion*, trans. M. J. Charlesworth (Notre Dame, IN and London: University of Notre Dame Press, 1965), p. 117. Anselm uses "supreme being" (*summum omnium solum*) in chap. V; in *St. Anselm's Proslogion*, pp. 120 and 121.

2   St. Anselm, *Proslogion*, chap. II, in *St. Anselm's Proslogion*, p. 117.

Knowing that God Is

It is another question whether one can know *that God is* and not love God. Say that one knows God as the Supreme Being who is infinitely good, merciful, loving, and powerful exists. Would such a person then love God? Anselm in the *Proslogion* used the ontological argument to prove, or try to prove, that God, the Supreme Being than which nothing greater can be thought, *must* exist. And, in chapter V, he argued that God, as that than which nothing greater can be thought, "is whatever it is better to be than not to be," and so has the traditional perfections.[3]

There has been much discussion of Anselm's ontological argument, and since its inception there has been controversy regarding its logical soundness. St. Thomas Aquinas in the thirteenth century rejected it because it assumes that human beings can know the essence of God.[4] But he agreed with Anselm that God's existence could be proven, just not with the ontological argument. God's existence could be proven, Aquinas thought, in "five ways," reasoning from God's "effects," which are evident in the world. Each of his five ways is a comparatively short argument, some shorter than the ontological argument, which is itself short. Unlike Anselm, Aquinas proved the existence of God as, for instance, a "first mover" (the first way) or a "first efficient cause" (the second way),[5] observing at the end of each argument, "this everyone understand to be God" or this everyone names as God or "speaks of" as God or "calls" God.[6] Aquinas did not think that God was *only* a first mover or first cause. He knew that those reading his arguments would fill in the attributes

---

3   St. Anselm, *Proslogion*, chap. V, in *St. Anselm's Proslogion*, p. 121.

4   St. Thomas Aquinas, *Summa Theologica*, I, q. 2, a. 1, in *Basic Writings of Saint Thomas Aquinas*, ed. Anton C. Pegis, vol. 1 (New York: Random House, 1945), p. 19.

5   *Efficient cause* is an Aristotelian category. Efficient causes are the mechanical movement-producing means in causation. A person who mixes paints is the efficient cause of the new pigment created.

6   St. Thomas Aquinas, ST, I, q. 2, a. 3, in *Basic Writings of Saint Thomas Aquinas*, pp. 21–24.

or perfections of God as part of his nature, and in any case he himself in the *Summa* filled out the "manner" of God's existence regarding, for instance, God's perfection, goodness, infinity, and eternity.[7] Aquinas, whose effort was in part to show that faith and reason are not in conflict, thought that those with adequate intellect could use their natural reason to follow his five ways of proving God's existence and so come to "scientific knowledge" (*scientia*) of God's existence, while others who were unable to follow his arguments could accept by faith God's existence.

Aquinas' five ways or arguments are also subject to controversy. Immanuel Kant (1724–1804) rejected them as well as the ontological argument.[8] Others too have criticized these arguments. Our issue is not the logical soundness of these, or any, arguments for God's existence. Our issue, as it relates to these arguments, arises when we note that if any such argument is sound, knowledge of God's existence is created. The issue before us is the relation between that knowledge and love of God.

The conclusion of a proof of God's existence is the proposition "God exists." If an argument for God's existence succeeds as a proof, it proves that this proposition is true. The resulting belief, the belief the proof justifies, is precisely the belief that there is a God, that God exists. At about the middle of the twentieth century the philosopher Norman Malcolm raised the question "Is it a religious belief that 'God exists'?" His answer was that it is not. The religious belief, Malcolm argued, is belief *in* God, typically animated by trust, not a belief *that* God exists. In fact Malcolm wondered if the latter could be any kind of belief at all.[9]

---

7   St. Thomas Aquinas, ST, I, qq. 4, 6, 7, and 10, in *Basic Writings of Saint Thomas Aquinas*, pp. 37–41, 51–62, and 74–84.

8   Immanuel Kant, *Critique of Pure Reason*, I Transcendental Doctrine of Elements, Second Part, Second Division, book II, chap. III, secs. 4 and 5, A592/B620–A614/B642, in *Immanuel Kant's Critique of Pure Reason*, trans. Norman Kemp Smith (Boston and New York: Bedford/St. Martin's, 1965), pp. 500–14. The first or A edition of the *Critique of Pure Reason* was published in 1781; the revised B edition was published in 1787.

9   Norman Malcolm, "Is It a Religious Belief that 'God Exists'?" in *Faith and the Philosophers*, ed. John Hick (New York: St. Martin's, 1964), pp. 106–07.

His appreciation that simply believing that God exists, without a response to God, has little or no religious engagement led Malcolm to say that the belief that God exists is not a religious belief. An episode in the life of Bertrand Russell appears to substantiate Malcolm's perception of the religious irrelevance of a sheer belief that God exists and as well the religious irrelevance of knowing that God exists. Russell, one of the foremost philosophers of the twentieth century, was for most of his life an atheist or agnostic. At one point, however, when he was twenty-two and studying at Trinity College, Cambridge something remarkable occurred to him. Here is his description.

> as I was walking along Trinity Lane . . . I saw in a flash (or thought
> I saw) that the ontological argument is valid. I had gone out to buy
> a tin of tobacco; on my way back, I suddenly threw it up in the air
> and exclaimed as I caught it:
>
> "Great God in boots! The ontological argument is sound."[10]

Russell sees, or thinks he sees, that the ontological argument works, it proves its conclusion. Thus, he believes, he now knows that its conclusion, God exists, is true. Does he thank God for what he has come to see or turn to God in devotion? He does not say, but presumably not. His reaction, we may assume, was to return to his rooms and make philosophical notes on the logic of the argument.

Several centuries before Malcolm John Calvin (1509–64) anticipated his thinking about belief that God exists. There are, Calvin said, "two kinds of faith." One kind is had "if anyone believes that God exists, or regards as true history that which he is told of Christ." The second kind is "when we believe, not only that God and Christ exist, but also believe in God and Christ." The first kind is "of no importance," Calvin says: it is held "in common with the devils," and Calvin cites James 2.19 ("You believe that God is one; you do well. Even the demons believe—and shudder"). Calvin counts as the first kind of faith belief that God exists, but also other beliefs-that about

---

10   Bertrand Russell, "My Mental Development," 1943, quoted in Ronald W. Clark, *The Life of Bertrand Russell* (New York: Alfred A. Knopf, 1976), p. 45.

the life of Christ, and he allows that this kind is real faith or belief. But he and Malcolm would agree that this kind of faith or belief is of no religious importance. The kind of faith that is religiously significant, they would agree, is belief *in*, or faith *in*, God. For Calvin, as opposed to Malcolm, this kind of faith includes but goes beyond belief that God exists; and for Calvin it explicitly requires trust, for it involves putting "all our hope and trust in one God and Christ."[11]

Calvin discussed two kinds of faith or belief. The point of his concern retains its force if the first kind of faith is understood to be, not belief, but knowledge, as his reference to James 2.19 indicates it could have been. The devils or demons to which James refers are acutely aware of God's existence; that is, within the story James is drawing on, they know very well indeed that God exists. Their reaction is fear—not awe, but stark fear. It is not love. If, on the other hand, one comes to know that God exists through the intellectual means of theological argumentation, then again one will not doubt that there is a God, but, as with Russell, one's religious response might be nil. The knowledge attained may have no affective reverberation whatsoever.

Malcolm came to appreciate that the bare belief that God exists is of no religious importance. Calvin understood that the more complex belief that God exists combined with beliefs about the history of Christ still is of no religious importance. Even if one following the ontological argument comes to believe, not only that God exists, but that God has all the perfections and so is infinitely loving, powerful, and good, as the ontological argument is supposed to prove, the resulting belief may be a belief of little religious importance, in the sense that it has no religious impact on one's life, as the case of Bertrand Russell's experience with the ontological argument indicates. The same is so if one believes that one knows, as Russell must have briefly thought, or *does* know, that God exists and has the perfections attributed to an all-powerful, all-merciful, and all-loving God.

---

11   John Calvin, *Institutes of the Christian Religion—1536*, chap. 2, in *John Calvin: Selections from His Writings*, ed. John Dillenberger (n.p.: Scholars Press, 1975), p. 274.

There appears to be a spiritual step between appropriating in belief or knowledge true propositions about God's nature or existence and turning in one's heart toward God.

III. TO KNOW GOD IS TO LOVE GOD

ST. PAUL SAYS in his first letter to the Corinthians that if one loves God, one is known by God (1 Cor. 8.3), but there is as well a religious sensibility that affirms that to know God is to love. John in his first letter says, "let us love one another, for love is of God, and he who loves is born of God and knows God. He who does not love does not know God; for God is love" (1 Jn. 4.7–8). For this religious sensibility the relationship of the believer to God is one of love. John is speaking of love of "one another." But this sensibility easily extends to love of God, so that if one loves God one knows God, and if one knows God with understanding one loves God. This religious sensibility, so understood, has been presented and discussed by D. Z. Phillips. The understanding that knowledge of God brings, he says, "is the understanding of love." For Phillips "to know God is to love Him." There is no knowledge or understanding of God apart from love of God; there is no "theoretical understanding of God."[12]

Phillips recognizes that people may reject the whole of religion as a way of life, and he recognizes that one (like Ivan Karamazov) may *defy* God without loving him. In fact he allows that there may be a number of affective responses to God by those who defy God without denying God's existence,

---

12   D. Z. Phillips. "Faith, Scepticism, and Religious Understanding," in *Faith and Philosophical Enquiry* (New York: Schocken Books, 1971), pp. 21, 26, and 29. Phillips has been termed a "non-realist" by John Hick (in *An Interpretation of Religion*, pp. 198–99). Hick calls Phillips a nonrealist because Phillips understands the reality of God exclusively in terms of the way the religious live their lives, as opposed to a reality that exists independently of ourselves. Phillips, like Malcolm, thought that the belief *that God exists* is not a religious belief, and belief or faith *in God* (traditionally trust in God) does not require a belief that God exists. Phillips' views on the love of God and knowledge of God, which is our concern here, are compatible with his nonrealist position, but may be treated independently of his general position.

including resentment and even hatred. But, he says, still "the love of God is the primary form of belief in God if only because the intelligibility of all the other attitudes . . . is logically dependent on it." That is, the affective attitudes of defiance, resentment, hate, as well as fear and rebellion, are understandable only as rejections of love of God.[13]

Phillips does not pursue the question of whether those who defy God without denying his existence understand and know God as do those who love God. He says only that they see "the story from the inside, but it is not a story that captivates" them.[14] What he is clear on is that there is no "theoretical understanding of God." Phillips' denial of "theoretical" theological understanding may, however, put him at odds with Aquinas and others, for whom there are many things that we can know about God because they can be proven by natural reason, such as God's existence, perfection, infinity, and eternity. A part of what Phillips is saying is that there is no intellectual mastery of the concept of God or theological arguments for God's existence and attributes on the basis of which one can love God. Many would agree that this is not the religious path. Beyond this Phillips may mean as well (1) that it is impossible to know God with understanding and not to love God, or even (2) that love is all there is—there is no knowledge of God apart from that love. Of course, if he means either (1) or (2), the existence of those who know that God exists but react with an attitude other than love, or with indifference, poses a difficulty. Perhaps, though, he and others with the religious sensibility of 1 John 4 would say that they do not really know God: knowing God is not a matter of knowing God exists or knowing true propositions about God, they might say. In any case there is a difference between (1) and (2). The (1) option allows that there is knowledge of God and that one could religiously come to know God with understanding of his goodness and mercy, but if one

---

13   Phillips. "Faith, Scepticism, and Religious Understanding," pp. 30–31. Phillips cites Malcolm's "Is It a Religious Belief that 'God Exists'?," in which Malcolm says that religious belief in God allows, in addition to trust, the other attitudes that he mentions.

14   Phillips, "Faith, Scepticism, and Religious Understanding," p. 31.

attains such knowledge it then becomes impossible logically, psychologically, or metaphysically not to love God. The (2) option in effect rules out any such knowledge of God by equating knowledge with love.

Phillips is not alone in having the religious sensibility he presents. Some with it, though, would distinguish between different types of knowledge of God. They would distinguish between different types in terms of content, separating knowledge of God's existence and simplicity, on the one hand, and knowledge of God's loving nature, on the other hand; or they would distinguish between any propositional knowledge about God, on the one hand, and knowing God himself and his love, on the other hand. They might also distinguish between different types of knowledge in terms of provenance, distinguishing between intellectually gained knowledge, gained through theological reasoning, and experiential knowledge, gained through experience of God. In the next section we will turn to experience of God and of God's love and consider the experiential knowledge that such experience implies.

IV. KNOWLEDGE OF GOD THROUGH EXPERIENCE OF GOD

ST. BERNARD OF CLAIRVAUX (1090–1153) wrote a series of sermons on the Song of Solomon, also known as the Song of Songs. In these sermons Bernard presented God's love as something that could be experienced. Much of the Song of Solomon is an amorous dialogue between a lover, the king (Song 1.4), and his beloved. Traditionally the Song is understood as an allegory expressing God's love for his people or, in the Christian tradition, expressing God's love for the church or God's divine love for the individual soul. In the Christian reading followed by St. Bernard, the king is the Bridegroom or Christ, and his Bride is the human soul. God's love, for Bernard can be experienced as the Bridegroom's love. Bernard's account is more than theoretical. It is autobiographical, for Bernard found in the Song a faithful echo of his own experience of God's divine love.[15]

---

15   St. Bernard of Clairvaux, "Sermons on the Song of Songs," in *Bernard of Clairvaux: Selected Works*, trans. Gillian R. Evans (New York and Mahwah: Paulist Press, 1987), pp. 210–78.

Bernard in his treatise *On Loving God* presents an experience of God and of God's love in a different but related way. In both cases, though, Bernard's understanding of the experience of God's love has implications for the love that is to be given to God in return in the relationship of love between God and the aspirant, and also for knowledge of God. In his treatise he says that "God is the cause of loving God . . . for he is both the efficient and the final cause."[16] In elaboration Bernard says that God himself "provides the occasion" for our love of him, "creates the longing" and "fulfills the desire." "His love both prepares and rewards ours," and, says Bernard, "Kindly, he leads the way" and "repays us justly."[17]

Bernard in *On Loving God* proceeds to describe four "degrees of love" that "man," or human beings, may have or aspire to.[18] In the first degree of love, which is the beginning stage of love and the lowest degree, "man loves himself for his own sake." This form of love "results in bodily love" and is "innate in nature." When such love becomes excessive it is constrained by the commandment to love your neighbor as yourself, which counsels us to deny our pleasures for the sake of the needs of others. And if the needs of others can be met only at the cost of not meeting our own needs, then we should give generously, for there "is no doubt that he [God] will come to your aid generously."

To love one's neighbor "with perfect justice," Bernard says, "it is necessary to be prompted by God." And to "love your neighbor with purity" you must "love him in God." "But," Bernard says, "he who does not love God cannot love in God." Bernard concludes that "You must first love God so that in him you can love your neighbor." If Bernard means explicit love of God, as he seems to, then the religious sensibility that he expresses here is, at least on

---

16   *Final cause*, like *efficient cause*, is an Aristotelian category. As the efficient cause is the moving or mechanical cause, the final cause is the purpose or end (*telos*).

17   St. Bernard of Clairvaux, *On Loving God*, in *Bernard of Clairvaux: Selected Works*, p. 191.

18   St. Bernard of Clairvaux, *On Loving God*, in *Bernard of Clairvaux: Selected Works*, pp. 192–97.

the surface, counter to the religious sensibility we discussed in the last section of the previous chapter.

Interestingly, Bernard discusses such love of neighbor with "purity" and "in God" under the heading of the first degree of love, love of oneself for one's own sake and benefit. Love of neighbor, for this love, finds an expression only in responding to the constraint of the commandment. In the second degree of love "man loves God for his good." Such love of God is "not only for his own benefit, but for himself," that is, for his greater good, beyond the desired benefits sought in the first degree of love. In Bernard's account of the first two degrees of love there is no reference to an experience of God or of God's love.

In the third degree of love "man loves God for God's sake," and in this degree of love there is the element of experience of God. In this degree it is necessary for one to "call upon God often and to taste by frequent contact," discovering "by tasting how sweet the Lord is." In this degree of love it is not difficult to keep the commandment to love one's neighbor, for one "truly loves God, and therefore he loves what is God's."

The fourth degree of love in which "man loves himself for the sake of God" is for Bernard rarely attained, but it also includes an experience of God. Perhaps, Bernard allows, "the holy martyrs received this grace while they were still in their victorious bodies—at least in part." Bernard speaks of the "experience of this kind of love" being such that the mind, "drunk with divine love," forgets itself and clings to God. But, for Bernard, to "lose yourself as though you did not exist and to have no sense of yourself," to become "almost annihilated," belongs to "heavenly not to human love." The fourth degree will be reached "when no entanglements of the flesh hold [one] back," although this does not mean that the fourth degree of love is utterly denied to persons in this life, only that such love is but briefly experienced. Bernard in describing the fourth degree uses the same metaphors that others have used to try to express mystical union with God. In this degree of love, in which "human affection" dissolves and is "poured into the will of God," it is as when "a drop of water seems to disappear completely in a quantity of wine" or as when a "red-hot iron becomes indistinguishable from the glow of fire" or as when "air suffused with the light of the sun seems transformed into the brightness of the light." "To love in this way," says Bernard, "is to become like God." But if "any mortal . . . rapt for a moment" is "admitted for a moment to this union," immediately he is called back by the world, "the day's wickedness," the needs of his "mortal body," "the weakness of his corruption," and, says Bernard, "more powerfully than these—brotherly love calls him back."

A question arises about the place of overt action, and the forms of that action, in the four degrees of love as Bernard understands them. We will take up the question of the place of action in the love of God in chapter 6. Here, though, we should note that as Bernard in his sermons on the Song of Songs allows an experience of God and of God's love, so too in his treatise *On Loving God* he recognizes an experience of God and of God's love. In his sermons on the Song of Songs God's love is experienced as the Bridegroom's "kiss of his mouth."[19] In *On Loving God* in both the third and the fourth degrees of love there is an experience integral to the love of God. As we saw, in the fourth degree of love Bernard speaks of one's being "rapt," if only for a moment, and in the third degree of love Bernard says, echoing Psalm 34, that by tasting one discovers the sweetness of the Lord. These experiences of God and of God's love provide a knowledge of God and of God's love, but do they also come to, or result in, love of God?

Bernard himself may not have thought so, for in a sermon he argues that God should be loved because he first loved us. Surely, Bernard concludes, "he deserves to be loved in return."[20] If there were a logically sound argument for the existence of God and his nature, including his love, anyone with wit enough could follow the argument and come to knowledge (*scientia*, or scientific knowledge, as Aquinas called it) that a loving God exists. But such knowledge might leave one unaffected. A similar point holds for Bernard's reasoning that God should be loved. Though one follows and agrees with

---

19   St. Bernard of Clairvaux, Sermon 2 on the Song of Songs, in *Bernard of Clairvaux: Selected Works*, p. 216.

20   St. Bernard of Clairvaux, Sermon 2 on the Song of Songs, in *Bernard of Clairvaux: Selected Works*, p. 175.

Bernard's logic, one might not be moved to love God. (A parallel case in human affairs that exhibits the same disconnection between cognitive conviction and affective response is when a person knows that the other in their joint effort deserves more credit, but cannot bring him- or herself to give it.) As with theological arguments for the existence of God, there is a gap between the knowledge they allegedly yield and the affect of a religious response, so with Bernard's argument there is a gap between accepting the conclusion that God deserves love and an actual response of love.

But perhaps Bernard's argument is not only ineffective but superfluous. Perhaps knowledge gained by or within the kind of experience Bernard relates in his treatise and especially in his sermons on the Song of Songs is different from knowledge gained by argument. Perhaps by its very nature it is affective. Experiencing God after all is very different from proving intellectually that God exists. (By analogy one may learn that there are rattlesnakes in the Mojave Desert by reading a brochure, but that is very different from learning that there are rattlesnakes in the Mojave Desert, and what it is like to encounter a rattlesnake, by having the experience of stepping on one.) If one comes to know God's love by experiencing God and God's love, an affective and emotional response may be so near the horizon of that experience that it merges with it. This possibility deserves examination, to which we now turn.

John Henry Newman and "Real Assent"

The contrast between religious knowledge gained by experience and by logical inference has been recognized by many. John Henry Cardinal Newman (1801–90) saw a difference between what he called "notional assent" and what he called "real assent" that in some ways parallels this difference. Newman's concern in *A Grammar of Assent* was with assent to propositions, or claims regarding the truth. In particular he was concerned with assent to "dogmas," or religious doctrinal propositions (about the Being and attributes of God, for instance). "To give a real assent" to a dogma, he said, "is an act of religion; to give a notional [assent] is a theological act." A real assent "is discerned, rested in, and appropriated as a reality by the religions imagination." A notional assent "is held as a truth, by the theological intellect."[21] Newman's distinction is not exactly the one that we have identified. For one thing he gives to "religious imagination" what may seem an inflated role. However, for him imagination relates to the use of images, and religious experience was and is formed by images. Bernard's experience of God as a Bridegroom uses an image in this sense. On this point, then, the difference may not be as great as it is regarding two other points. Newman is treating an assent to *propositions*, and our concern is knowledge of God, knowing God, and its relation to loving God. One form of knowledge of God is, to be sure, propositional, as we have seen. Knowing that "God exists" is knowing that that proposition is true. But knowing God is other ways is not purely propositional. These other forms do not reduce to knowledge of propositions about God. Knowing God through religious experience of God or of God's love is to experience and know God, as opposed to knowing things *about* God. Second, Newman's concern is with *assent* to propositions, and assent is not knowledge. Many forms of assent to the truth of a claim do not come to knowledge. Nevertheless, Newman, like many other religious writers, was aware of the vast difference between what in broad terms is intellectual acceptance and a contrasting religious acceptance grounded in some form of experience.

Bernard's experience of God as the Bridegroom of the soul is not the only form that religious experience of God or God's love can take. Julian of Norwich (c. 1342–1416) provides another model for such experience: the experience of "Mother Jesus" as a loving God who loves her/his children regardless of their failings.[22] And there are other forms of the experience of God in accord with other images, as well as the tasting of God that Bernard refers to. When there is a religious experience of God, however, the affective

---

21   John Henry Newman, *An Essay in Aid of a Grammar of Assent* (Notre Dame, IN and London: University of Notre Dame Press, 1979), p. 93. *A Grammar of Assent* was first published in 1870.

22   Julian of Norwich, *Showings*, Long Text, chap. 61, in *Julian of Norwich: Showings*, trans. Edmund Colledge, O.S.A. (New York; Ramsey, NJ; and Toronto: Paulist Press, 1978), p. 301.

response may not be love. As one can experience God as a Bridegroom or as a loving Mother or a Good Shepherd, so one might experience God as a stern Judge. When God is experienced in this last way the affective response may well be closer to fear (not awe, but stark fear) than to love. Yet as there can be a religious experience of God so there can be a religious experience of God's love, and it is an evocation of an experience of God's love that we find in Bernard's and Julian's writings.

St. Paul, as we noted earlier, says that the love of Christ surpasses knowledge, but he says this in the expression of his prayer that the Ephesians may "know the love of Christ which surpasses knowledge" (Eph. 3.19). Here "know" means "experience," as in "May you know what it is to be loved." Such experience brings with it knowledge by acquaintance, though what it is of— Christ's love or God's love—in its nature surpasses propositional knowledge. Furthermore, though one can know God's love through experiencing it, one will not thereby gain a knowledge of the nature of God's love if Paul is right, for such knowledge surpasses human understanding.

If one experiences God's love, and so comes to know it through acquaintance, will one then love God? To say to know God's love is to love God is different in subtle ways from saying to know God is to love God. Yet both raise the issue of the relation between knowledge and love. Love is a response to the one who is loved. Clearly in flesh-and-blood human love relationships the one who is loved and loves in return must in some manner know the one who is loved through some form of acquaintance. That acquaintance may be minimal. In a human love relationship it might be an epistolary acquaintance, and it might be inaccurate or false in the beliefs it instills. Yet in human relationships there must be some acquaintance with love's object. Even when the object of one's love is imaginary, there is a felt sense of acquaintance. The idea of love without an object of love, as only an affective state, or "state of mind," we examined in chapter 2. As a characterization of romantic love it is deficient, we saw. Love of another person, or of God, is relational. It requires an object. Love of God is *of God*. *Implicit* love of God, it was argued in the previous chapter, does not require belief in God; even more so it would not require knowledge of God. Love of God may be implicit, in accord with the religious sensibility that we drew on in the previous chapter, reaching God through a love of creatures. Nevertheless it is relational, being love *of* God. But if it is *explicit* love of God it requires an acquaintance with, or awareness or knowledge of, God.

However, while explicit love of God presupposes some kind of knowledge of God as that to which one's love is given, that knowledge may be minimal, as it may be minimal in human love relationships. Perhaps all one can say or think is that God is the Supreme Being or the Greatest Reality or that presented in the scripture of one's religion. Or experientially one may love that whose presence one has found in aspects of one's life with no further conceptual specification. Such an explicit love of God is intelligible. But also it may be that many have experienced the presence of God and his love in their lives without recognizing it as the presence of God and his love, and if so they will not have responded with either belief in God or love of God. Even if an experience of God's love involves an affective response, that response may not be love of God. It may be only a sense of elation, nearly devoid of a religious dimension.

Thus while explicit love of God requires some form of knowledge of God, different forms of knowledge and experience of God and even of God's love do not necessitate love of God. The question remains: Is there a form of knowing God or knowing God's love that makes not loving God impossible? If there is such knowledge of God it will join immediately and seamlessly to love of God (if it is distinguishable from love of God). It will be a knowledge that can deepen, as understanding can deepen and as love can deepen. If there is such a knowledge of God or of God's love it would have to be profoundly felt, as St. Bernard of Clairvaux and Julian of Norwich profoundly felt, and so felt they knew, God's love, and this means that in some way it would have to be experienced, attained by experience or given to experience. It is worth noting that the images of God's love used by Bernard and Julian are of human love that is experienced and naturally returned with alacrity. A bride's love of her bridegroom—Bernard's image—is natural and spontaneous and returns the bridegroom's love. A child's love of his mother—Julian's image—is natural and spontaneous and returns his mother's love. Of course these images as images of God's love presuppose religious belief, and in these images the love that is experienced, and in this way known, is yet distinguishable from the love that is returned. Still, perhaps these images of God's love capture what is true in the identification of knowing God and loving God: a natural and spontaneous response to an experience of knowing God's love is a return of that love.

Chapter Five

The Command to Love

I. INTRODUCTION

IN THE JEWISH AND CHRISTIAN TRADITIONS there is a commandment to love God with all your heart and soul and there is a commandment to love your neighbor as yourself. In the Islamic tradition the Qur'anic expectation that the faithful will love God is clear, as when we are told that if any among those who believe turn from the faith, God will bring others to replace them and

> He will love [them]
> As they will love Him. (5.57)

We noted in chapter 2 that the Qur'an speaks of the righteous giving food to the poor, the orphan, and the captive out of love for God. For Judaism and Christianity God's commandments tell us what God expects of us. They tell us what we ought to do religiously and morally—or religiously, if not morally. The command to love creates a religious duty to love, and for believers all ought to love as God commands. In these traditions love is not to be given reluctantly merely out of a sense of duty (if it is possible to love reluctantly); yet those who fail to love fail to do as they ought. Using a term that is not exclusively religious but is most at home in religion, those who fail to love their neighbors sin against God and against their neighbors. Those who fail to love God and their neighbors sin against God by violating their relationship to God in failing to love God and their neighbors, if for no other reason than disobedience; and those who fail to love their neighbors sin against their neighbors by violating their proper relationship to their neighbors, religiously conceived. The sin in failing to love is in not doing as we ought in our relationships to

God and to our neighbors, and what we ought to do is expressed in God's commandments to love.

Such, in one construction, is the religious understanding in the theistic religions of the Abrahamic traditions that recognize God's commandments to love. But the idea that we can have a duty or obligation *to love* has seemed to many to be misguided and even deeply wrong in its conception—as opposed to a duty to help and do good for others—whether it is a duty to love God or our neighbors, or anyone. There are reasons for this animadversion, and in this chapter we will address those reasons.

A main source of the problem that many see with a command to love relates to the interior dimension of love. In earlier chapters we have noted the interior, affective dimension of love. Love has as well an exterior, active dimension, and in section II of this chapter we will consider the necessity of both dimensions for a full expression of love.

In section III, drawing primarily on the reflections of Immanuel Kant, we will identify and illustrate the moral perspective that rejects the coherence of an obligation, and of a command, to love.

For this moral perspective the imperative to love does not and cannot function as a moral imperative. To posit love as a moral principle, for this perspective, is a scandal in its incoherence. In section IV we will discuss wherein that scandal does and does not lie.

Finally, in section V, we will focus on the moral intuition that is at the core of the rejection of an obligation to love. As we will see, it is an intuition that many take to be evident and that may well be right. In the fifth section we will examine two very different ways that religion might relate the command to love to this moral intuition.

II. THE INTERIOR AND EXTERIOR DIMENSIONS OF LOVE

THE RECOGNITION of an interior and an exterior dimension in the explicit love to be given to God is long standing in Christian spirituality. St. Aelred in the twelfth century distinguished between *affectus mentis* (interior affection) and *effectus operis* (external works) in the love of God. *Effectus*, for Aelred, takes the form of the practice of the virtues, while *affectus* consists in "the sweetness of spiritual taste."[1] Aelred's reference to the "spiritual taste" of God is close to St. Bernard of Clairvaux's language in his treatise *On Loving God* and in his presentation of the Bride's yearning for the Bridegroom in his sermons on the Song of Songs. This should not be surprising, for St. Aelred was a contemporary of St. Bernard and like Bernard was a Cistercian. Both were abbots, Bernard of Clairvaux in France, Aelred of Rievaulx in England. Meditation, for Aelred, belongs to the interior dimension of *affectus*, while reading, interestingly, belongs to the exterior dimension of *effectus*, as it encourages virtue.[2]

Another instance of the recognition of the two dimensions of the love of God is provided by St. Francis de Sales (1567–1622) in his *Treatise on the Love of God*. He identified "two principle exercises of our love towards God, the one affective, the other effective." The first, de Sales says, "consists principally in prayer." It involves an activity, but an interior activity. The second is more active, and in following this exercise of love for God one serves God through "the inviolable obedience requisite to effect the ordinances of the divine will."[3] Both Aelred and de Sales in effect identify two ways of loving God. However, all love of God, as love, will have both an interior and an exterior dimension, even though one may be given emphasis over the other.

The two aspects or sides of love are evident in the biblical commandments of love themselves. The first commandment is to love God with all your heart and soul. In its very statement in the Torah and New Testament this first commandment speaks to the interior lives of those who receive it, for it calls for an orientation of one's heart and soul, and therefore of one's feelings and thoughts. And it relates to exterior action as well. We may be sure that we know God, John tells us in his first letter, "if we keep his commandments"

---

1   Simon Tugwell, O.P., *Ways of Imperfection: An Exploration of Christian Spirituality* (Springfield, IL: Template Publishers, 1985), p. 108.

2   Tugwell, *Ways of Imperfection: An Exploration of Christian Spirituality*, p. 108.

3   St. Francis de Sales, *Treatise on the Love of God*, trans. Henry Benedict Mackey, O.S.B. (Westport, CT: Greenwood Press, 1945), bk. VI, chap. I, p. 231.

(1 Jn. 2.3). The active or exterior dimension of love for God, in accord with what de Sales wrote, is expressed in actively keeping God's commandments or ordinances. The second commandment, to love your neighbor as yourself, also has both exterior and interior dimensions. In the parable of the Good Samaritan, the Samaritan actively cares for the man who needs his help, rendering physical aid, but he also acts out of compassion. The roots of both the exterior and interior demands of love for others are in the Jewish tradition. In the Torah we find the divine instruction that "you shall not harden your heart against your poor brother" who is in need. "You shall give to him freely when you give to him" (Deut. 15.7 and 10). In order for one to love one's brother or neighbor one must do more than give of one's wealth. One must give from the heart with feeling for the other.

Yet a recognition of the interior and exterior dimensions of love is not distinctly religious and does not rely on the authority of religion, although religious traditions like Judaism and Christianity may particularly heed the distinction. Independently of the religious recognition of these two dimensions, their recognition is evident in the way we in our untutored lives regard various expressions of love between persons. Consider a parent's love for his or her child. If a parent was merely beneficent toward her child, caring for his needs and providing for him, but doing so disdainfully, we would judge the parent's love to be deficient, if we allowed that it was love at all. Such a parent might be acting solely out of a sense of moral duty without an interior affect of caring. Conversely, if a parent was overflowing with loving feeling toward his child, abundantly expressed, but though able to did not provide for his child's physical needs and support, we would again judge that there was a deficiency in love.

Thus there need be no appeal to a special religious concept of love to find an interiority of love that compliments love's exterior expression. Each is necessary in our everyday understanding of what it is to love another person, and the two dimensions are related such that, if one is lacking, it is made impossible or questionable that the dimension that is present may be called an expression of love, or at least it is made questionable whether it is an expression of love as love should be. At least in this respect religious love of God and of neighbor is like love between persons outside religion.

III. IS THERE A DUTY TO LOVE?

LOVE BETWEEN PERSONS, as we have observed, is valued in every culture, but this does not mean that there is either a moral or a religious obligation, or duty, to love. To be sure in Judaism and Christianity there are commandments to love God and our neighbors, and hence a duty to love; but the mere fact that love in human relations is valued does not in itself mean that there is an obligation to love. In fact, Immanuel Kant rejected the idea of an obligation or duty to love if love is understood to have an interior dimension.

Immanuel Kant

For Kant there is a supreme principle of ethics, which he called "the categorical imperative." It is this: "Act only according to that maxim whereby you can at the same time will that it should become a universal [moral] law."[4] Kant thought that if a person was contemplating an action such as making a false promise (his example) and could not rationally "will" it as a universal moral law, so that it would be allowable for everyone, then it was a wrong action. There are questions about how exactly Kant's categorical imperative is to be applied and about its relations to other basic moral principles that he promulgated, which he apparently regarded as alternative formulations of the categorical imperative. These questions, however, need not detain us. What we should note is what Kant says about two kinds of duties that he recognized, moral duties that one has to oneself and moral duties that one has to others. He says,

> One is accustomed to calling these obligations, respectively, the duties of self-love and love of one's neighbor; but these expressions are not taken here in their proper meanings, for there can be no

---

4   Immanuel Kant, *Grounding for the Metaphysics of Morals*, second section, 421, in *Immanuel Kant: Ethical Philosophy*, trans. James W. Ellington (Indianapolis, IN: Hackett, 1983), p. 30, in book I. Kant's *Grundlegung zur Metaphysik der Sitten* is also given other titles in English, including *Groundwork of the Metaphysics of Morals*. It was originally published in 1785.

direct duty to love, but only to act so that one makes himself and other men his end.[5]

For Kant there can be no "direct duty to love." He clarifies this comment when he turns his attention to duties to others. After identifying a "principle of *mutual love*," which directs human beings "constantly to approach one another," and a contrasting "principle of *respect*," which directs human beings "to keep themselves at a distance," he says this about love.

> Now, *love* is not understood here as feeling (sensitive [*ästhetisch*]), i.e., as pleasure in the perfection of other men, nor, accordingly, as complaisant love (for there can be no obligation to have feelings). Instead love must be thought of practically, as the maxim of benevolence; and this maxim results in beneficence.[6]

For Kant we can and do in one way have a duty to love others. It is the ethical duty of benevolence or beneficence to others. It is the duty to *act* beneficently so as to do good for others. The only duty to love that Kant recognizes is the duty to act in a loving way, or beneficently, in accord with the exterior dimension of love. Regarding the interior dimension, Kant is clear, there is no duty. As he asserts, "there can be no obligation to have feelings."

John Stuart Mill

The utilitarian ethics of John Stuart Mill (1806–73) are fundamentally opposed to Kant's ethical theory. For Kant, though our actions may have good or bad effects, the consequences of what we do are irrelevant to the

---

5   Immanuel Kant, *The Metaphysics of Morals*, part II, The Metaphysical Principles of Virtue, I The Elements of Ethics, First Part: Concerning Duties to Oneself, 410, in *Immanuel Kant: Ethical Philosophy*, p. 70 in book II. *The Metaphysics of Morals* was originally published in 1797.

6   Kant, *The Metaphysics of Morals*, part II, The Metaphysical Principles of Virtue, I The Elements of Ethics, second part: Concerning Ethical Duties to Others, 449, in *Immanuel Kant: Ethical Philosophy*, p. 113 in book II (emphasis in the original).

moral rightness of our actions. For Mill, in accord with the principle of utility, or "the greatest happiness principle," the good or bad consequences of what we do—the pleasure and pain our actions produce—determine the moral rightness of our actions. Although Mill believed that a feeling for "the good of others" may become for an individual "a thing naturally and necessarily to be attended to," Mill did not say that individuals had an obligation to have or to act on such a feeling.[7] Mill agreed with Kant that moral duty applies to our overt actions and not to our feelings. Neither Kant nor Mill appeals to God's command to love. Their effort, like many who follow in their respective moral traditions, was to ground ethics philosophically. If they had considered the religious command to love, understood as requiring love in both its interior and exterior dimensions, it is clear that they would have rejected its import regarding a duty to love.

St. Bernard of Clairvaux

St. Bernard, who of course recognized God's command to love, shares in a way worth noting Kant's perception of the great difference between a command or duty to *act* in love and a command or duty to have the *feelings* of love. Yet his treatment of the duty to love as it relates to the interior dimension of love is very different from Kant's.

A straightforward reading of the New Testament and of the Torah is that we *are* to incline our hearts in love. We are to love God with all our heart and soul. In the parable of the Good Samaritan, Jesus presents the Samaritan as giving aid to the man set upon by robbers out of compassion—from his heart. "Love," says Bernard, reflecting his recognition of love's two dimensions, "is expressed in action and in feeling." However, the love that is commanded is much more clearly "love in action," for Bernard: "I believe," he says, that "men have been given a law, a settled commandment" to love in action. Love in feeling or sensation presents a contrast for Bernard. While we can in this

---

7   John Stuart Mill, *Utilitarianism*, ed. George Sher (Indianapolis, IN: Hackett, 1979), chap. II, p. 7, and chap. III, pp. 31–32. *Utilitarianism* was originally published in 1861.

life by "divine grace" experience the beginning of love in sensation, and even its progress, Bernard is clear that "it is fully known only in the happiness of the life to come." So, he asks, "How then were things which could not in any way be fulfilled made commandments?" "Or," he allows in reply, "if you would rather say that it is the sensation of love which is commanded, I do not disagree, so long as you agree with me that it can never and never will be possible for any man to fulfill it." By "commanding what was impossible he made men, not prevaricators, but humble," so "accepting that command . . . we shall cry to heaven and God will have mercy on us." Bernard is most comfortable with the command to love in action, but in his way he does not rule out a commandment and duty regarding the interior dimension of love, although, paradoxically, human beings will never be able to keep it.[8]

For Kant it is impossible to respond with the feelings of love, and so there is no duty to have the feelings of love. For Bernard too it is impossible fully to respond with the feelings of love, but still he allows that this may yet be commanded and so be a duty. For Bernard God in his wisdom has given us a command, the impossibility of keeping which has the religious value of making us humble and will bring us to turn toward God and call on his mercy.

IV. THE SCANDAL OF THE COMMAND TO LOVE

TO LOVE IS A COMMAND. But as a religious or moral command love is a moral scandal for many, for it does not operate as a normative principle should. Moral principles, we like to think, tell us what we ought to do or ought not to do. "Tell the truth" and "Do not steal" are imperatively expressed moral principles (as well as religious commandments), but "Love others" is not, it may seem, for it lacks specificity about what one should do to love. Moral principles, it seems, need specificity in order to be followed. And here we might think of moral casuistry as a paradigmatic effort to bring specificity to moral demands, or, as an even better example, we might think of the Jewish understanding and

---

8   St. Bernard of Clairvaux, Sermon 50 on the Song of Songs, in *Bernard of Clairvaux: Selected Works*, trans. Gillian R. Evans (New York and Mahwah, NJ: Paulist Press, 1987), pp. 241–42.

elaboration of the law—God's law, the Torah—as an effort to make specific the demands of the moral and religious law. In the Torah God provides the 613 commandments, and the *Halakhah* is a legalistic and logical elaboration of them in an effort to gain specificity. However Rabbi Elliot Dorff shows us that within Jewish thought, while there are different ways of understanding the halakhic process of the law, it need not be understood as a deductive process akin to geometry.[9] As Dorff sees it, within the Christian tradition among Catholics there is an emphasis on "institutional authority," and among Protestants an emphasis on "individual conscience," while in the Jewish tradition moral decisions are arrived at "through the instrumentality of Jewish law" and a "legal process."[10] That process, though, does not amount to a "deductive system." There is, for one thing, an interaction between Jewish law and custom. Dorff illustrates this interaction with the example of the treatment of women's issues by the Conservative movement (of which he is a part). In the twentieth century, in accord with the changing social roles of women, the Conservative movement recognized the ordination of women as rabbis.[11] Dorff observes that the Talmud is more argument, counterargument, and qualification than systematic deduction from apodictic principles.[12] Methodologically, even in Orthodox Judaism legal decisions about the law can be tempered. Rabbi Dorff recounts the following story.

In the early part of the twentieth century his grandparents were members of a large Orthodox synagogue in Milwaukee, whose rabbi was Rabbi Solomon Scheinfeld, the rabbinic head of the Orthodox community in Milwaukee. His grandparents often had guests from the congregation on the Sabbath. One Friday afternoon, his father, then a boy of fifteen, was sent by Dorff's grandmother to ask the rabbi when the guests would arrive. When his father entered Rabbi Scheinfeld's office he was deciding whether a chicken was kosher. The

---

9   Elliot N. Dorff, *For the Love of God and People: A Philosophy of Jewish Law* (Philadelphia, PA: The Jewish Publication Society, 2007), pp. 48 ff.

10   Dorff, *For the Love of God and People: A Philosophy of Jewish Law*, p. 211.

11   Dorff, *For the Love of God and People: A Philosophy of Jewish Law*, p. 257.

12   Dorff, *For the Love of God and People: A Philosophy of Jewish Law*, p. 56.

rabbi examined the chicken and asked the woman who had brought it several question about the health and economic condition of her husband and family. Finally he pronounced the chicken kosher. After the woman had left, Dorff's father asked the rabbi why he had asked all those questions, to which Rabbi Scheinfeld replied, "If you think that the kosher status of chickens depends only on their physical state, you understand nothing about Jewish law."[13]

What Dorff's story shows is that in what Dorff calls the "legal process" of the elaboration and specification of Jewish law the procedure is neither deductive nor rigid. This is true as well in the Catholic tradition, in which pronouncements of the Church specify and clarify the principles that are to guide the behavior of believers, and in the Protestant tradition, in which there is a greater emphasis on individual conscience guided by scripture and God's inspiration. Immanuel Kant with his categorical imperative and John Stuart Mill with his utilitarian principle are closer to positing a deductive moral system. Each provides an axiomatic primary principle from which moral judgments can be deduced. Kant's categorical imperative operates as such a primary principle, and Mill's principle of utility does as well. Mill's principle of utility tells us that right actions produce the maximum of "general happiness," understood as pleasure and the absence of pain. If one action out of several that might be chosen maximizes happiness, then it follows that it is the right action without qualification.

Kant and Mill provide deductive systems, but this is not to say that all the moral principles or judgments they would want to deduce from their systems will have specificity, not if they want their systems to sanction all the general moral judgments that seem right to our pretheoretical moral sense. For many of those judgments lack specificity, such as "Help those in need" or "Be generous" or "Practice honesty." What will be helpful, generous, or honest will be greatly influenced by the context. What is helpful will depend on particular needs. What is generous in one situation may not be in another. As in Rabbi Scheinfeld's application of Jewish law, much beyond "the physical state of the Chicken" may be relevant. Allowing that there is a moral requirement to love,

---

13   Dorff, *For the Love of God and People: A Philosophy of Jewish Law*, p. 227.

as there is for many, its lack of specificity in particular situations, therefore, would not distinguish it from a range of moral judgments or principles.[14]

The scandal of the command to love, which is a command that is recognized in the Jewish tradition and in the Christian tradition in its Catholic, Protestant, and other expressions, is not that it cannot be deduced from a moral axiom or that it lacks specificity. The scandal lies in its interior content. For both Kant's deontological and Mill's utilitarian ethics the exclusive focus is on overt action. Even when Mill considers virtue and rights he analyses them in terms of their "general utility" or their "conduciveness to pleasure," focusing on overt actions that respect rights and that are virtuous.[15] And for Kant, virtuous actions are right actions done out of respect for the moral law. For both Mill and Kant, and many who follow in their moral traditions, love as a disposition of the heart is a moral nullity.

Finally the scandal of the command to love and what leads Kant to deny that there is a duty to love is its interior character. However, there is a deeper nucleus to the Kantian perception, which is not limited to Kant's moral perception and arguably exists in pretheoretical morality. We will turn to it in the next section.

V. LOVE IS FROM THE HEART

ONE CAN BE BENEFICENT and do good for others reluctantly, wholly out of a sense of duty, without any great feeling for those being helped. Beneficence is a matter of actually helping others, not a matter of feeling. It is for this reason that Kant allowed that it could be a duty. The interior dimension of love, though, *is* a matter of feeling. Fully to love others is to act from the heart.

---

14   The subject here is the specificity, or lack of it, of moral principles and judgments. Once the moral demands of love are determined in a particular case, it would remain, as we saw in regard to the parable of the Good Samaritan in chapter 3, that there may be a real and great difference between the ethical or moral demands and the religious demands of love.

15   Mill, *Utilitarianism*, chaps. IV and V, pp. 37 and 52.

Love cannot be given without the spontaneous feelings of love. But can we have an obligation to have spontaneous feelings?

Kant said, "The action to which the *'ought'* applies must indeed be possible under natural conditions."[16] His pronouncement correlates with a familiar moral intuition that in ordinary parlance is often expressed as "ought implies can"—we have an obligation to do only what we can do, what is voluntary and within our power to do. And if it is not within our power, we cannot be expected to do, or to have done it. Obligation and our responsibility do not extend to it. Our feelings, Kant perceived, are involuntary and beyond our control, and so obligation does not extend to them. The moral intuition that "ought implies can" is as much a nuclear or core intuition in pretheoretical morality as in Kantian ethics, and so, if our feelings are beyond our control, this reasoning is not purely Kantian but applies in pretheoretical morality as well.

There are two religious reactions or sensibilities that face this moral intuition. The first is that our feelings are not under our control, but still we are responsible and blameworthy. This is the reaction of St. Bernard. It is also the reaction of the contemporary religious philosopher Robert Merrihew Adams, who argues that there are "involuntary sins." One such involuntary sin, for Adams, is anger, not angry behavior, but the feeling or state of mind of anger. In addition to being responsible for the voluntary expressions of our anger, we are also responsible for the feeling of anger that descends upon us involuntarily, as we are for such feelings of jealousy or hatred, as well as certain "corrupt beliefs" and "wrong desires" that we cannot control.[17] For this religious sensibility those who fail to have feelings of love are yet responsible and blameworthy for this failure, even though it is involuntary. This reaction, then, rejects the validity of the moral intuition that ought implies can.

---

16   Kant, *Critique of Pure Reason*, I Transcendental Doctrine of Elements, second part, second division, book II, chap. II, sec. 9. III, A548/B576, in *Immanuel Kant's Critique of Pure Reason*, p. 473.

17   Robert Merrihew Adams, "Involuntary Sins," *The Philosopher's Annual*, vol. 8 (1985), pp. 1 and 2.

The second religious sensibility agrees with the first, that we are responsible for our feelings but regards our feelings as being sufficiently under our control. This second religious reaction accepts the moral intuition that ought implies can. It accepts that we can incline our hearts, and it accepts the apparent implication of the command to love God and neighbor—that such love is something we can bring about in ourselves, perhaps with God's help, in love's exterior and interior dimensions. It may be that we cannot instantly redirect our hearts to feelings of love, as one can in an instant decide to tilt one's head, but, for this religious sensibility, we can endeavor to incline our hearts and over time, perhaps with God's help, succeed in reorienting our hearts to the disposition and feelings of love. St. Bernard, who insisted that "the sensation of love" cannot be "fully known" in this life, and so that it is not possible to *fulfill* the command to have feelings of love, nevertheless did not deny that through divine grace we can experience the beginning and even the progress of such feelings. Bernard did not explicitly say that it was within our power to open ourselves to feelings of love, but if he saw "divine grace" as helping human endeavor, he would allow that divinely assisted human effort could attain the beginning of such feelings.

These two religious reactions, in their very different perceptions of our control of our feelings, have their moral counterparts. On the one hand, we morally allow that at times strong emotions are beyond our control. But when they are, in contradistinction to Adams' view of involuntary sin, we allow diminished moral responsibility and blame, as when one does something in the heat of the moment in the grip of anger or rage, as opposed to doing it with calculation. On the other hand, we give such moral advice as, "Loosen up," "Don't be so guarded. Be more spontaneous." And we issue such moral imperatives as "Don't be so selfish," "Don't be angry," and "Be more sympathetic." All of these, at least in part, relate to a person's interior life and feelings, and impute control over such feelings.

In St. Paul's letter to the Ephesians he says, "Be angry, but do not sin; do not let the sun go down on your anger" (Eph. 4.26), which may be understood as relating to the exterior actions of anger and allowing the involuntary character of the feeling of anger. Yet he also says, "Let all bitterness and wrath and anger ... be put away from you" (Eph. 4.31), which is more in accord with the second religious sensibility and its sense that we are responsible for controlling our feelings; although, to be sure, each passage could be interpreted such that it sanctioned either the involuntary or the voluntary view of our feelings. What is religiously unquestioned and recognized by both the religious sensibilities we have consulted is that the command to love relates to both the exterior and the interior dimensions of love.

IN THE JEWISH AND CHRISTIAN TRADITIONS there are the command to love God and the command to love one's neighbor. Indeed these two commandments are central to Christianity. But these commands are perplexing in that it seems they cannot be kept in the interior dimension of love. As we have seen in this chapter, in religion—specifically within the Christian tradition—there are different reactions to this perplexity. For one religious sensibility, though our feelings are beyond our control we are yet responsible for them, and we sin when we fail to have feelings of love. For another religious sensibility, we do have adequate control over our feelings, and if we do not have feelings of love, we are responsible for that reason. That there are commands to love God and one's neighbors in both actions and feelings is accepted by both sensibilities. For believers, if we fail to love we fail to do as we ought, we fail in our religious duty and sin. But if we keep the commandments by loving solely out of a sense of duty, do we truly love God or our neighbor? We will address this question in the next chapter.

Chapter Six

Love of God

I. INTRODUCTION

THE ASYMPTOTE OF LOVE is the asymptote of human love, the love that human beings experience for one another. The endpoint that this asymptote approaches is uttermost love, a love that may be utterly unlike commonplace human love. The infinite endpoint of love, love in its highest form, in the theistic traditions is God's love. In our early discussion we first identified kinds and styles of love that are quite human, some all-too-human, we might think. Yet recognizing them as love was necessary. As our discussion continued we turned to a form of love that is closer to the endpoint approached by the asymptote of love, love of others as love of neighbor. We now turn to a form of love that is for theistic believers closer yet to the infinite endpoint approached by the asymptote of love: explicit or implicit love of God.

However, it will be recalled, even before we turned to love of others in chapter 3 we had found several issues or questions that relate to uttermost love or to that love that begins to approach uttermost love. What are its "works"? How will it be expressed? Will it be rational or reasonable? Will it entail denial of self? And what will it love? We will turn to the question of what makes love reasonable in chapter 10. In chapter 2 we discussed self-denial in *agapeistic* human love; we will take up the question of the place of denial of self in love that approaches uttermost love in chapter 9. The question of all that will be loved by uttermost love, or the love that begins to approach uttermost love, will be addressed in chapter 8, where we will consider the scope of such love. In the present chapter we will take up the first two questions—What are its "works"? and How will it be expressed? Also, there is a question about loving God out of a sense of duty. As one's neighbors will be loved so, for believers,

73

God is to be loved. As there is a commandment to love our neighbors, so there is a commandment to love God. This raises the question: Can one love God, or one's neighbor, as a response to duty? This question does not ask Can there be a duty to love? That was the question of the previous chapter. The new question asks Can one love as a matter of duty? We will address this question in section II.

Whether as a response to duty or not, what are the "works" of love of God, and how is love of God expressed? Or, as it has been put, what are the signs of love of God? As we will see, within Christian thinking at least since the Middle Ages there has been a concern about knowing with certainty that one loves with religious love. This issue, furthermore, as we will see in section III, relates to both the inner and outer dimensions of explicit love of God.

Nevertheless religious writers, including St. Bernard of Clairvaux and St. Francis de Sales, have recognized, in broad terms, ways of loving God, and we will consult their reflections in section IV.

In section V we will turn to the question of what it means to love "in God" and "for the sake of God."

And in section VI we will consider possible expressions of love of neighbor and of God, and possible concrete works of the love of neighbor and of God in a modern recognition.

II. CAN LOVE BE A RESPONSE TO DUTY?

AS THERE IS in the Jewish and Christian traditions a command to love, to love one's neighbor and to love God, so for these traditions there is a duty to love. In the previous chapter we encountered the question of whether one can have a duty to have the feelings of love when, allegedly, our feelings are not subject to our control. Whether our feelings of love are or are not within our control, we saw that the religious perspectives of the two religious sensibilities we examined is that the command to love extends to both love's exterior, active dimension and its interior, feeling dimension. This understanding, which abides in both the Christian and Jewish traditions, entails that there is a duty to love both actively and within our hearts.

But now another question arises: *Can* one love as a response to duty? If we fail to love as we are commanded to do, then we fail in our religious duty, for we fail to do as we ought to do. This much is clear, if not to Kant at least to the religious perspective. The newly arisen question, though, presents a new issue. If we somehow succeed in loving our neighbors or God, but do so solely as a matter of duty, would that "love" truly be love?

St. Paul, referring to the "Gentiles," wrote to the Romans that "what the law requires is written on their hearts" (Rom. 2.15). Paul's words echo Jeremiah's that the Lord says, "I will put my law within them, and I will write it upon their hearts" (Jer. 31.33). The Gentiles were those outside the Jewish tradition, but presumably for Paul the requirements of God's law are written on every heart. By extrapolation the requirements of love are written on our hearts, that is, made a part of our internal moral or religious understanding, for, given what Paul says, the requirements of the two great commandments, to love neighbor and God, as a part of the law would then be written on our hearts. In fact in the Christian tradition all the law depends on these two commandments (Mt. 22.40). In this way the requirements of love of neighbor may be given to our internal understanding, and even when we do not explicitly act for the sake of God's commandment (of which many may not have heard) we may, in accord with what is written on our hearts, respond to others with love. The parable of the Good Samaritan shows what it is to act as a neighbor, and Jesus offers it to illuminate the commandment to love our neighbors. The Samaritan who acts as a neighbor in Jesus' parable acts out of compassion for his neighbor in need. Jesus does not say that the Samaritan acts for the sake of God's commandment or out of duty to observe God's commandment.

And what of the first commandment, to love God? Can the "Gentiles," or those who have no thought of God and even do not believe in God, love God by responding to what is written on their hearts? We have already seen that for an identifiable religious sensibility they will be able to, for a love of God may be expressed through a love of our neighbors. If Paul is saying that the requirements of both of the great commandments are written on our hearts, then his letter to the Romans arguably contains the same recognition.

We find in the parable of the Good Samaritan more reason to think that the requirements of love are written on our hearts and so infused into our moral or religious sense. In the parable, as we have seen, when Jesus asks his hearer "Which of these three"—the two worthy members of the community who passed by the man who had been robbed and beaten, and the Samaritan who stopped and cared for his needs—"proved neighbor to the man?" he replies that it was the one who showed mercy (Lk. 10.37). He can draw on the intuitions of his heart to identify the Samaritan as the one who showed love for his neighbor. And this is so even though if he had himself encountered the man set upon by robbers quite probably he, like the two worthy members of the community, might have followed conventional morality and passed him by.

If the requirements of love are written on our hearts and so inform our deepest moral or religious sense, then our response of love need not have its source in a response to duty to keep a commandment to love. But say that one's love does have its source in a response to duty to keep a commandment to love. Will one's "love" be love? There are strong reasons to think that at most it can be only a facsimile of love. Love of others, it has been argued, requires a response to them. A response to the duty to love others as our neighbors, however, is distinct from a response to others. Similarly, a response to the duty to love God is distinct from a response to God. Religious love as *agape* is a response to others, or to God, while a response to a duty is a response to a moral or religious duty.

The fundamental difference between these two responses ramifies into two further reasons why love given as a response to the duty to love can only be a facsimile of love. First, a reluctant or a grudging giving is compatible with acting out of a sense of duty: all that is required is that the obligation be kept, reluctantly or otherwise. Love, on the other hand, cannot be given in this manner. Reluctance undermines and ultimately disproves love. Second, the affect of the facsimile of love engendered by a sense of duty is wrong. Consider a person who loves his or her neighbor or God solely out of fear of punishment if he or she does not love. His or her concern is with avoiding punishment, not with those he or she is to love or with God. The concern of one who loves solely out of a sense of duty is similar. It is a concern with doing as she or he ought and not a concern with those she or he is to love or with God. One may deeply desire not to be punished and one may deeply desire to do as one ought, but if these desires constitute the affection of one's heart, there is not the response to others or to God that is the response of love. This is not because religious love has a unique demand. It is because love for others demands what it does. So it is that one can marry another for the other's money, but one cannot love another for the other's money, although with a different kind of love one can love the other's money.

There is, then, a paradox in the command to love. In the Jewish and Christian traditions there is a command and hence a duty to love, but if believers love as they are commanded merely out of a sense of duty to keep the commandment, they will fail to keep the commandment either to love their neighbors or to love God. Love must be given from the heart. This is the religious perception, and it is a perception that is not confined to religion. Can one endeavor to so incline one's heart? As we have seen, at least some among the religious would say so, although, they may say, only with God's help. Can the religious out of a sense of duty endeavor to incline their hearts to love others and to love God? It would seem so, but if they succeed in coming to love their love will not be given from a sense of duty.[1]

III. THE ELUSIVENESS OF RELIGIOUS LOVE

IN THE MIDDLE AGES it was felt that one could not be certain that one's own, or others', love was indeed religious love or charity (*caritas, agape*). Still, it was felt, there could be signs or indications (*signa*) that one's love was genuinely charity, though such signs must be inconclusive. Though inconclusive, they

---

1   One may recall here Pascal's parallel point about unbelievers who have become intellectually convinced that religious belief is in their self-interest, but the state of their emotions prevents them from believing. They should begin by doing as believers do— taking holy water, having masses said, and so on—which, Pascal thought, would bring them in a natural way to full and committed belief. Blaise Pascal, "Infinity-Nothing: The Wager," *The Pensées*, trans. J. M. Cohen (Harmondsworth, UK: Penguin Books, 1961), p. 158. Pascal wrote his *pensées*, or thoughts, in the seventeenth century.

amount to possible "works" or expressions of the love of God. The French Dominican William Perault, or Peraldus (c. 1190–1271), offered a list of *signa* of charity or love for God, several of which are as follows:

> we enjoy thinking about God
> we enjoy being in God's house
> we enjoy talking about or with God
> we enjoy listening to God's word
> we enjoy practicing generosity for his sake
> we endure hardship for his sake
> we obey God's commandments[2]

St. Thomas Aquinas, who was Peraldus' contemporary, in his *De veritate* (or *Truth*) recognized as signs of charity one's being ready "to undertake spiritual works" and that one "effectively hates evil."[3] It is interesting that the list of signs offered by Peraldus, and the signs named by Aquinas, are centered on overt activity. One of the *signa* on Peraldus' list is obeying God's commands, which, as we noted in chapter 2, is, along with thanking God, "always and for everything" a way of believers loving God that even nonbelievers could see in the behavior of believers. The same comment holds for the other *signa* offered by Peraldus, even thinking about God to the extent that such thoughts are expressed. As Simon Tugwell says, "the emphasis is on *doing* certain things."[4]

Although Aquinas' two signs relate to overt behavior, his reflections on the elusiveness of love extend to the interior dimension of love as well. Aquinas says of one who may, or may not, have charity that he "cannot know from the act of love which he perceives within him[self] whether he has reached the stage where he is united to God in the way which is needed for the nature of

---

2   Simon Tugwell, O.P., *Ways of Imperfection: An Exploration of Christian Spirituality* (Springfield, IL: Template Publishers, 1985), p. 144. Tugwell, p. 150n43, cites Peraldus' *Summa de Virtutibus*.

3   St. Thomas Aquinas, *De veritate*, q. 10, a. 10, "Can One Know that He Has Charity? in St. Thomas Aquinas, *Truth*, trans. James V. McGlynn, S.J. (Indianapolis, IN and Cambridge, UK: Hackett, 1954), vol. 2, p. 56.

4   Tugwell, *Ways of Imperfection*, p. 144 (his emphasis).

charity." Aquinas allows that one may know with certainty that one loves "a brother," but still he will not know with certainty that that love is charity.[5] This may sound like the uncertainty of the young man who asks himself, "Do I really love her, or is this only infatuation?" For Aquinas, though, the uncertainty regarding charity arises even when it is clear that some form of love is present. It is uncertain whether one's love is charity because charity's "immediate object and end is God" and this makes "that to which charity is ordained" beyond our comprehension, for we cannot discern God to be the object and end of our love.[6] As Tugwell paraphrases Aquinas' point, it is that there is a "psychological impossibility of distinguishing with certainty between natural and supernatural motivation."[7]

Aquinas, we should observe, though he regards the immediate object and end of charity to be God, does allow that there can be charity for "a brother," that is, for others, and thus recognizes more clearly than Peraldus religious love of one's neighbors. Also Aquinas allows that one "who has charity can surmise that he has charity from probable signs," such as the two he names.[8] Such a probable surmise would not amount to certainty, but it could be a confident belief, we may suppose. It would of course be counter to the religious requirement of humility pridefully to proclaim that one has perfect charity, or pridefully to believe that one does, but this is because such an assertion or belief flows from self-concerned pride. Aquinas even allows that one can know with certainty that one has charity—if "it be revealed to him by God."[9]

More importantly for our present concern we should be clear that the point of these medieval thinkers is not that religious love of God or neighbor—charity—is impossible. It is that it is impossible for one to know that one has charity (unless it is revealed by God). One's love may be charity even if

---

5   St. Thomas Aquinas, *De veritate*, q. 10, a. 10, in *Truth*, vol. 2., p. 57.

6   St. Thomas Aquinas, *De veritate*, q. 10, a. 10, in *Truth*, vol. 2, p. 56.

7   Tugwell, *Ways of Imperfection*, p. 144.

8   St. Thomas Aquinas, *De veritate*, q. 10, a. 10, in *Truth*, vol. 2, p. 56.

9   St. Thomas Aquinas, *De veritate*, q. 10, a. 10, in *Truth*, vol. 2, p. 56.

one cannot know that it is. One's surmise that one's love is charity may be correct. Aquinas does not deny this point and even clearly allows it when he says that one "who has charity can surmise that he has charity." Thus even if medieval thinking about the elusiveness of charity is correct (and the point of this section is neither to affirm nor to deny that it is correct), the possibility of religious love of neighbor and of God is not thereby called into question.

IV. EXTERIOR AND INTERIOR WAYS OF LOVING GOD

THOUGH THERE IS the viable theological idea that one cannot be certain one has charity and though this idea may furthermore be grounded in a religious sensibility (which may exist independently of Aquinas' rationale), more than one religious thinker has reflected on the exterior and interior ways of loving God. Peraldus' listed signs of charity, understood as signs of love for God as opposed to love for neighbors—as Peraldus seems to have understood them— may be seen as essentially exterior ways of loving God.

In the previous chapter we drew on the discussion of St. Francis de Sales in his *Treatise on the Love of God* to show his awareness of both the interior and exterior dimensions of love and of the love of God. In that discussion de Sales distinguishes between interior—affective—and exterior—effective— ways of loving God. For de Sales the primary interior way of loving God is through prayer. Peraldus, we saw, lists "talking about or with God" as a sign of charity. The Dominican Order is the Order of Preachers, and as a Dominican Peraldus would recognize talking about God in preaching; he also recognizes talking with God, by which he means prayer. If Peraldus means *saying* prayers, his meaning is not quite what de Sales has in mind. By prayer de Sales means the more interior and affective activity of contemplative prayer. On the active side of love de Sales names "inviolable obedience" in keeping God's commandments. For Peraldus too obeying God's commandments is a way of loving God, assuming that the signs he names may be understood as not just possible but actual expressions or ways of loving God.

St. Bernard of Clairvaux in regard to the third degree of love says of one at this level of love that he "truly loves God, and therefore he loves what is

God's." He finds it easy to keep the commandment to love one's neighbors. "He loves chastely, and to the chaste it is no burden to keep the commandments; the heart grows purer in the obedience of love."[10] Here there is the idea that love of God is expressed in keeping God's commandments with spontaneous obedience, the same idea expressed by de Sales. Bernard even calls it the "obedience of love." De Sales and Bernard mean explicit love of God, for the obedience they have in mind is explicit obedience of God's commands recognized as such.

As we have seen, one may love God through loving others according to a certain religious sensibility. In chapter 3 we saw that this sensibility recognizes an implicit love of God through loving others even when there is no thought of God. Now, though, it emerges that there can also be a love of God through loving others when the love of God is explicit. Bernard and de Sales do not mention, and in what they explicitly say neither deny nor affirm, the possibility of loving God through the love of others. Nevertheless Bernard and de Sales, like Paul in his letter to the Romans, both in effect recognize a love of God through loving others. They do because for both of them one way is to keep his commandments is to love our neighbors. Thus it is not only for the religious sensibility that looks to the parable of the King in Luke but also for St. Bernard of Clairvaux and St. Francis de Sales, and the more traditional understanding they represent, that God may be loved through loving others. Loving God through loving others is *implicit* love of God if there is no thought of God, but *explicit* love of God if there is a belief in God and a turning toward God in obeying his commandments.

Such love of God through the love of others, whether implicit or explicit, will and must have the affective or inner dimension of love. It will not take the form of Bernard's experience of "the kiss of his mouth," for this is an experience of God's love for oneself, as is Julian of Norwich's experience of being loved by Mother Jesus. Its interior dimension will be in an affective concern

---

10   St. Bernard of Clairvaux, *On Loving God*, in *Bernard of Clairvaux: Selected Works*, trans. Gillian R. Evans (New York and Mahwah, NJ: Paulist Press, 1987), p. 194.

for others, those through whom God is loved implicitly or explicitly. Mother Teresa of Calcutta (Kolkata) explicitly loved God and Christ, but she found Christ in every suffering and dying person that she aided and loved.

And as there need be no thought of God for either the active or inner dimension of implicit love of God, there is no reason why those in nontheistic traditions cannot be seen by those in theistic traditions as implicitly loving God, not by virtue of what they believe but by virtue of those they love and how they love (at the same time those in a Buddhist tradition may see compassionate Jews, Christians, and Muslims as implicitly seeking Buddhahood). As the asymptote of love progresses toward its endpoint the cognitive burden of love may lessen.

V. FOR THE SAKE OF GOD

IN WHAT ST. BERNARD IDENTIFIES as the third degree of love, as we saw in chapter 4, one loves God for God's sake. This seems understandable. For whose sake would explicit love of God be, if not for God's sake? In the fourth degree of love one loves oneself, but for the sake of God. This is harder to understand. The closely related idea that we are to love our neighbors for the sake of God is equally hard to understand.

Must charity or love of a neighbor be for the sake of God in order to be love? Might not charity be love for the sake of the human person who is loved? If we love our neighbors could it not be for their sake? In fact shouldn't it be? Or, if charity is love for the sake of God, could it not be for the sake of God *when* it is for the sake of human persons, as the parable of the King (Mt. 25.34–40) suggests as strongly as it suggests that one can love God through loving others?

St. Thomas Aquinas in what we have quoted from his *De veritate* does not deny that we can love God through loving others. Strictly, even if Aquinas is right that the object and end of charity is God, so that charity is for the sake of God, and right that one cannot know if one's love reaches God in union with God, the possibility that one can love God through loving others is left completely open. It may still be true that one's love reaches that end—God—through loving others. But will they be loved if they are not loved for their own sake?

Loving others but not for their sake brings us back to Nygren's view of *agape* (charity). It makes love of one's neighbor something other than a response to one's neighbor. And if loving our neighbors is a response to the duty to love our neighbors, and not to our neighbors, we are back to the problem we examined earlier in this chapter. Not loving our neighbors out of compassion for them, as we argued earlier, is counter to the parable of the Good Shepherd.

How then is loving for the sake of God to be understood? One way is to understand love for the sake of God as requiring belief in God along with the conscious directing of our love to God alone. Let us, though, explore another way of understanding love for the sake of God informed by a different religious sensibility. St. Bernard's fourth degree of love is love of oneself for God's sake. In it, as we saw in chapter 4, you "lose yourself." Extrapolating from St. Bernard's category, we might also say that love of others will be love for God's sake if in loving others one loses oneself, and in *agape* for others one does lose oneself at least to an extent in setting aside self-concern. Such love *is* of others but also of God if one's "intention is toward God" we may say, following a religious sensibility expressed by Meister Eckhart (c. 1260–1328). Meister Eckhart says of "whoever really and truly has God, he has him everywhere." He, or she, "has only God, and his intention is toward God alone, and all things become for him nothing but God."[11] In St. Bernard's terms in such love one loves one's neighbors "in God." For Eckhart if one "has God" one can love God for his sake in loving his brother, for all things have become God. This is not loving others as a means of loving God so that others are not loved for their sake. As in the parable of the Good Samaritan love of neighbor responds to the needs of others in love for them for their sake, and for this

---

11   Meister Eckhart, *Counsels on Discernment*, trans. Edmund Colledge, O.S.A., Counsel 6. "Of detachment and of the possession of God," in *Meister Eckhart: The Essential Sermons, Commentaries, Treatises, and Defense*, ed. Edmund Colledge O.S.A. and Bernard McGinn (New York; Ramsey, NJ; and Toronto: Paulist Press, 1981), p. 251.

religious sensibility *it thereby becomes love of God for his sake*. St. Bernard, read in accord with this religious sensibility, in seeing the fourth degree of love as love of oneself for God's sake—and by extension love of others for God's sake—sees that when we religiously love others for their sake with an abandonment of self-concern we love them in God or for God or for the sake of God, or, in Eckhart's language, with an intention toward God.

In this way the two commandments that we love God with all our heart and soul and love our neighbors as ourselves are seen to be seamlessly united. This is the perception or sensibility that Johann Arndt (1555–1621) expressed in *True Christianity* when he said, "The love of God and the love of neighbor are one thing and must not be divided."[12]

The importance of loving for the sake of God and the issues it raises belong to the theistic religious traditions, particularly to the Christian tradition. They have no purchase in the nontheistic traditions, although a close analogue does. In Buddhism one is to have compassion for all sentient beings and one is to seek *nirvāna*. The analogous issue for Buddhism is: Can one have compassion for the sake of attaining *nirvāna*? The analogous issue for nontheisitic Hinduism is: Can one follow the demands of dharma (duty) or the *advaitist* way of knowledge for the sake of *moksha* or release?

VI. LOVE OF NEIGHBOR AND GOD: WORKS AND EXPRESSIONS

WE SEE, then, that in various strains of religious sensibility it is recognized that God can be loved through loving others, and that God can be loved when others are loved for the sake of God. This brings us to the question of how God is to be loved through loving others. All love of others, and *agape* or charity in particular, responds to others or to another. What are the ways of implicitly or explicitly responding to God through responding to others? The parable

---

12   Johann Arndt, *True Christianity*, chap. 24, "On the Love of God and Neighbor," in *Johann Arndt: True Christianity*, trans. Peter Erb (New York; Ramsey, NJ; and Toronto: Paulist Press, 1979), p. 126.

of the King in Matthew 25 gives us some idea of a Christian response to this question. There, as we saw in chapter 3, the king tells the righteous that they gave him food when he was hungry, drink when he was thirsty, clothed him when he was naked, visited him when he was sick or in prison when they did these things for the least of his brethren.

These are expressions of *agape* or charity, or the religious love that demands no return, which begins to approach uttermost love. They are among the different ways of expressing or manifesting concern for others that transcends family, clan, caste, or close personal associations. Such love may be given individually, as in the case of the Good Samaritan, or socially within one's community or nation or even internationally. Given a broad scope, it may take the form of working for famine relief or in response to the needs of victims of floods or earthquakes half a world away. It may take a form not emphasized or ever contemplated in the first centuries of the Common Era or before, such as seeking to alleviate the suffering from disease through a scientific endeavor to find a cure for such scourges as malaria, bilharzia, or AIDS or in the effort to distribute existing medications to the sick and diseased. In another form it may pursue justice for those denied justice, that justice which prophets like Isaiah and Amos (Is. 28.17 and Amos 5.15 and 6.24) so often exhorted those who heard them to practice. In a contemporary setting a pursuit of justice might take various forms, including legal revision and the protection of civil rights. In the social arena the expression of *agape* may also express itself in the effort to open avenues to the realization of persons' potential, or to provide education for deprived minorities or slighted majorities, or in efforts to oppose war and violence.

All of these endeavors of course could fail to be expressions of love, as they would if they were pursued solely for the sake of reputation or self-aggrandizement, as they could be. They would also fail as an expression of love, as we have seen, if pursued solely out of a dedicated sense of duty. Doing good for others, or beneficence, can be pursued as a matter of duty—the point that Kant keenly appreciated—but doing good for others is not love. It corresponds to the exterior dimension of love at best, and the exterior dimension without the inner side of love is not fully love. The affective side of course need not be dramatic in its expression, as often it would not be in, for instance, working to organize food shipments for famine relief or in the daily routine of a research scientist systematically seeking the cure for a crippling disease.

Also, we should appreciate, religious love in the form of *agape*, a giving love that demands no return, can be evinced in a "normal" life. One need not be an Oxfam worker. One may have religious love for those one is close to, those in one's family or clan or caste, and when religious love is manifested in such close relationships its affective side will be more in evidence. Religious love of family, though, is essentially love of neighbor. It cannot be the biased love sanctioned by conventional morality that gives a point to the New Testament teaching that we must "hate" our father and our mother. The lack of bias in religious love, as well as a human tendency toward biased love, is recognized in Judaism and Christianity, but not in these traditions alone. In the teachings of Buddhism we are to have compassion for all others, indeed for all sentient beings; however, as the Dalai Lama has observed, we often are "biased toward our families and friends."[13]

One way to love God for St. Francis de Sales and more widely in the Christian tradition is through the interior practice of prayer. This way is open to those in the Western theistic traditions, to those in the *bhakti* tradition of Hinduism, and in the form of prayers to the *bodhisattva* Avalokitśvara or to Amida Buddha to those in some forms of Buddhism.. De Sales recognized prayer as one of the "two principal exercises of our love toward God." That it is not the focus of this chapter's discussion does not diminish its importance as a traditional way of loving God. In addition there may be a range of more or less individualized ways of loving God, involving prayer, meditation, and devotion in various combinations with active benevolence embodied in service to others.

The second "principle exercise of our love toward God" identified by de Sales has been our focus. It is the more active way of loving God, although this is not to say that it lacks an interior dimension, for it cannot anymore than an

---

13   His Holiness the Dalai Lama, *Ethics for the New Millennium* (New York: Riverhead Books, 1999), p. 69.

interior way of loving God can wholly exclude the active dimension, a point on which St. Teresa of Ávila was quite clear.[14] The attention we have given to more active ways of loving God has allowed us to contemplate the close connection between the commandment to love God and the commandment to love our neighbors as ourselves. For identifiable strains of religious sensibility we may love God and love God for his sake through loving our neighbors. In this way the love of God becomes as present and palpable as the love given to fellow human beings, for the love of God is expressed in that very love.

---

14   St. Teresa tells us that in the Prayer of Quiet, a peace is given in which one's will is "united with its God," which leaves "the other faculties ... free to busy themselves with His service," so that this "great favour ... unites the active life with the contemplative." St. Teresa, *Ways of Perfection*, chap. XXXI, in *Complete Works of St. Teresa*, trans. E. Allison Peers (London: Sheed and Ward, 1972), vol. 2, pp. 128–29.

Chapter Seven

God's Love

I. INTRODUCTION

GOD'S LOVE, the love that God gives to his beings, in theistic traditions is the zenith of love and in this book's terms it is the infinite endpoint of the asymptote of love. But how is God's love to be conceived or understood? What is its nature? How is it to be known, and can it be known? In this chapter we will pursue these questions, drawing on religious sensibilities and theological reflection. Within the theistic religious traditions it is possible to speak of a God relationship, the relationship between believers, or an individual believer, and God. Such a relationship may be a faith or trust relationship, or a relationship defined by obedience or devotion or by all of these orientations to God together. Faith, trust, obedience, and devotion characterize the way that the believer relates to God, or strives to relate to God, not the way that God relates to the believer. Love is different. In theistic traditions the believer is to love God, but also believers and indeed all of God's children and beings are loved by God. Love defines a religious relationship in which believers and God both give and receive love.

In chapter 2 we looked at overt expressions of believers' love of God discernible to all, and in the preceding chapter we looked at ways of loving God that are given religious recognition. In this chapter we will look at the love relationship between believers and God through a different lens, focusing on how believers find, respond to, and experience God's love. The main concern of this chapter will be to examine the different ways the religious present to themselves and understand God's love.

Yet for some God's love is beyond human understanding. In fact there are two broad and divergent ways in which the religious may approach God's love and other attributes of God, such as his goodness. One approach sees the attributes of God as beyond human language and comprehension. The other allows that God's attributes, and his love in particular, are in some measure open to human understanding. These two approaches are reflected in two contrasting religious sensibilities, and these sensibilities are the subject of section II.

These contrasting religious sensibilities and their two approaches to understanding God's love and other attributes inform two very different theological treatments of God's attributes. These opposed theological treatments will be examined in section III.

In section IV we will look at various ways that God's love is experienced by the religious in the Christian tradition, as well as at different images of God that provide avenues to both experience of God's love and ways of understanding the character of God's love.

The category of God's love can have no place in a nontheistic religious tradition. Yet it or its close analogue does have a place in some forms of Buddhism and Hinduism, as we will see in section V.

II. TWO RELIGIOUS SENSIBILITIES

FOR THE WESTERN THEISTIC RELIGIOUS TRADITIONS God is loving. In the Qur'an we find the following:

> But ask forgiveness
> Of your Lord, and turn
> Unto Him (in repentance):
> For my Lord is indeed
> Full of mercy and loving-kindness. (11.90)

In the Psalms, shared by the Jewish and Christian traditions, God's steadfast love is many times referred to, as when the Psalmist exclaims to God, "I will rejoice and be glad for thy steadfast love" (Ps. 31.7) and as when we are told that "his steadfast love endures for ever" (Ps. 100.5). In the New Testament Jesus says to "Love your enemies and pray for those who prosecute you" and not to love only "those who love you." And, he says, "You, therefore must be perfect, as your heavenly Father is perfect" (Mt. 5.43, 46, and 48). Here Jesus enunciates the idea that human love is to strive to be the love that God gives to human beings.

God's love is given universally and is steadfast, but beyond this what is its character? Religiously there are two contrasting ways to think about God's love (and other attributes). One way is to think of God's love as beyond human comprehension and conception. The other way is to think of God's love as significantly like and understandable in terms of human love. Both religious strains are found in religious sensibility as well as in theological thought.

Many believers have the sensibility that God is surrounded by mystery. The ways of God are not our ways. God's wisdom, goodness, and majesty surpass our understanding. God's ways and what God is are, for this religious sensibility, too great for our understanding. Properly we are in awe before God, and our words fail us. In the Psalms we find

> The heavens are telling the
>   glory of God;
> and the firmament proclaims his
>   handiwork.

But

> There is no speech, nor are there
>   words;
> their voice is not heard. (Ps. 19.1 and 3)

In the New Testament we read that the love of Christ "surpasses knowledge" (Eph. 3. 19).

Yet there is also the contrasting sensibility that we are to follow God's way, which requires that God's way be clear enough that it can be followed. God's mercy is to be welcomed, God is to be thanked for his manifold goodness, and God's majesty is to be praised. God's love is steadfast and in it we can find support and comfort. For this sensibility we can speak of God's mercy, goodness, majesty, and love, recognizing their greatness. This contrasting sensibility, as we will see, complements the first, despite some tension. Both sensibilities together may in many cases inform particular religious lives.

III. TWO THEOLOGICAL TREATMENTS OF GOD'S LOVE

GROUNDED IN THESE TWO RELIGIOUS SENSIBILITIES are two divergent theological treatments of God's nature and attributes, including God's love. The first is to be found in the mystical apophatic tradition, which espouses the ineffability of God. The second theological approach presents a way to make God's love and other attributes humanly understandable.

Dionysius and the Tradition of Ineffability

A primary and seminal author in the apophatic tradition is the fifth- or sixth-century author Dionsyius (or Pseudo-Dionysius), the same Dionysius who identified *agape* with *eros*. In *The Divine Names* he says that "we must not dare to apply words or concepts to [the] hidden transcendent God," although he does allow that "the Good is not absolutely incommunicable to everything." "By itself," he says, "it generously reveals a firm, transcendent beam, granting enlightenment proportionate to each being, and thereby draws sacred minds upward to its permitted contemplation, to participation and to the state of becoming like it."[1] Such a divine communication, though, like the voice of the heavens and firmament in Psalm 19, is wordless. In another briefer work, *The Mystical Theology*, Dionysius says the following about "the transcendent Cause of all things":

> What has actually to be said about the cause of everything is this. Since it is the Cause of all beings we should posit and ascribe to it all the affirmations we make in regard to beings, and, more appropriately we should negate all these affirmations, since it surpasses all being.

That is, we may both affirm and deny that God is this or that, is loving for instance, for in the case of God,

---

1   Dionysius, *The Divine Names*, chap. 1, 2, 588C, in *Pseudo-Dionysius: The Complete Works*, trans. Colm Luibheid (New York and Mahwah, NJ: Paulist Press, 1987), p. 50.

we should not conclude that the negations are simply the opposites of the affirmations but rather that the cause of all is . . . beyond every denial, beyond every assertion.[2]

Because our concepts do not apply to God both affirming and denying that God is this or that does not result in contradiction.[3]

Dionysius qualifies this severe thesis somewhat, as when he allows that certain "infinite names," like "Holy of Holies" and "Lord of lords," can be applied to God in praise in an "absolute sense," and as when he asks rhetorically,

> Is it not closer to reality to say that God is life and goodness rather than he is air or stone? Is it not more accurate to deny that drunkenness and rage can be attributed to him than to deny we can apply to him the terms of speech and thought?[4]

Nevertheless, his primary theological stance is to deny that words and human concepts apply to God. Our meager human conceptions, including *love*, cannot begin to capture what is true of the transcendent God, who is beyond all conception. For a theological approach informed by Dionysius' thinking, God's love, the infinite endpoint of the asymptote of love, is so far beyond human understanding that it cannot be named by "love."

St. Thomas Aquinas

St. Thomas Aquinas (1225–74) offers a very different theological view of God's attributes, and of God's love in particular, which is in accord with the second

---

2   Dionysius, *The Mystical Theology*, chap. 1, 2, 1000A-B, in *Pseudo-Dionysius: The Complete Works*, p. 136.

3   C. E. Rolt in his translation has "there is no contradiction between affirming and denying." *Dionysius The Areopagite*, trans C. E. Rolt (London: SPCK, 1940), p. 193.

4   Dionysius, *The Divine Names*, chap. 12, 1 and 3, 969A and 969C and *The Mystical Theology*, chap. 3, 1033C–D, in *Pseudo-Dionysius: The Complete Works*, pp. 126 and 140.

religious sensibility that we identified. For Aquinas, although we cannot intellectually "see" the divine essence, we can meaningfully predicate of God his significant perfections and attributes, including his love, which we come to know in a manner through creation and creatures, including our human existence. He allowed that "*good, wise,* and the like," which would include *loves,* can be applied to God "substantially," for, though they "fall short of representing Him," they "signify the divine substance."[5]

They are not metaphors but apply "properly," or literally, expressing God's perfections "absolutely" and "affirmatively," though not fully. For Aquinas we can know God and his perfections, including God's love. This "knowledge of God is derived from the perfections which flow from Him to creatures." However, these perfections—such as wisdom, goodness, and love—are in God "in a more eminent way."[6] Though "loves" may fall short of fully representing God, and though our knowledge of God's "eminent" degree of love may be wanting, we can yet know that God is love and predicate love of God "absolutely" in an "analogous sense." According to Aquinas' doctrine of analogical predication when we say, for instance, that a person is good and that God is good "good" is used in an "analogous sense," the goodness of creatures being "proportioned" to God's more excellent goodness.[7] The same applies to God's love.

Aquinas, then, is clear that believers can affirm God's love, meaning love in a literal, or "proper," sense, although that sense is analogical. For Aquinas in ordinary religious discourse believers may speak of God's love in praise and in thanks. God's love is not beyond the meaning of ordinary religious language. Human intention is important for meaning for Aquinas. At one point he argues that "God is good" does not mean "God is the cause of good things,"

---

5   St. Thomas Aquinas, *Summa Theologica*, I, q. 11, aa. 1 and 2, in *Basic Writings of Saint Thomas Aquinas*, ed. Anton C. Pegis, vol. 1 (New York: Random House, 1945), pp. 113 and 114–15.

6   St. Thomas Aquinas, *Summa Theologica*, I, q. 11, aa. 2 and 3, in *Basic Writings of Saint Thomas Aquinas*, vol. 1, pp. 114 and 116–17.

7   St. Thomas Aquinas, *Summa Theologica*, I, q. 11, a. 5, in *Basic Writings of Saint Thomas Aquinas*, vol. 1, p. 120 (emphasis deleted).

on the grounds that this is not the "intention" or the intended meaning "of those who speak of God."[8] He could as well have cast his argument in terms of the difference in meaning between "God is loving" and "God is the cause of love." When believers say that God is good or loving they mean to predicate goodness or being loving of God.[9] In the section of the *Summa* on God's love (ST, I, q. 20) Aquinas says,

> by the fact that anyone loves another, he wills good to that other. Thus he puts the other, as it were, in the place of himself, and regards the good done to him as done to himself. So far love is a binding force, since it joins another to ourselves, and refers his good to our own. And in this way too the divine love is a binding force, inasmuch as God wills good to others.[10]

Here Aquinas allows that the sense in which God loves is very like the sense in which one person loves another. Though only "analogous," as Aquinas would say, they are close. Aquinas was aware that we learn what goodness and love are in our lives as "creatures," in our human relationships. God's love is that love more eminently. God's love for Aquinas, then, may be understood as God's eminent love reached toward by the asymptote of human love.

IV. EXPERIENCE AND IMAGES OF GOD'S LOVE

OTHERS HAVE SEEN an analogy between human love and God's love. Using different images of God and of God's love they provide in another way an understanding of the nature of God's love.

---

8   St. Thomas Aquinas, *Summa Theologica*, I, q. 11, a. 2, in *Basic Writings of Saint Thomas Aquinas*, vol. 1, p. 115.

9   This of course is not to say that Aquinas denied that God is the cause of goodness or love. For Aquinas God is the cause of goodness and love, as well as being good and loving.

10   St. Thomas Aquinas, *Summa Theologica*, I, q. 20, a. 1, Reply to Obj. 3, in *Basic Writings of Saint Thomas Aquinas*, vol. 1, p. 217.

St. Bernard of Clairvaux

St. Bernard of Clairvaux in the century before Aquinas wrote a series of sermons on the Song of Solomon, or the Song of Songs. In chapter 4 we had occasion to consider his reflections on the experience of God and of God's love as he presented it in those sermons. Here we will further consider the nature of God's love as Bernard's experience presents it. The Song of Solomon is in the form of a courtly love song, overtly passionate and sensuous. The book begins with:

> The Song of Songs, which is
> > Solomon's.
> O that you would kiss me with
> > the kisses of your mouth!
> For your love is better than wine. (Song 1.1–2)

Much of the Song is an amorous dialogue between a lover, the king (Song 1.4) and his beloved, and as we remarked earlier, it is traditionally understood as an allegory expressing God's love for his people or, in the Christian tradition, expressing God's love for the church or God's divine and loving interaction with the individual soul. For St. Bernard, the king is the Bridegroom or Christ and his Bride is the human soul.

St. Bernard was a Cistercian monk and the Abbot of Clairvaux. Though he was strongly ascetic and committed to the monastic life, his spirituality gave an important place to religious experience, especially the soul's experience of God's love. Bernard found in the Song a faithful echo of his own experience of God's divine love. In his sermons on the Song, the soul's Bridegroom is "Jesus Christ our Lord, who is God" or, in another designation he uses, "the Word."[11] In a sermon that he begins with a passage from the Song, "All night long in my little bed I sought him whom my soul loves" (Song. 3.1), he says,

---

11   St. Bernard of Clairvaux, Sermons 74 and 84 on the Song of Songs, in *Bernard of Clairvaux: Selected Works*, trans. Gillian R. Evans (New York and Mahwah, NJ: Paulist Press, 1987), pp. 255 and 278.

"It is a great good to seek God."[12] The soul seeks God, yearns and "thirsts" for God.[13] As Dionysius finds yearning in the Wisdom of Solomon, so Bernard finds it in the Song of Solomon, where indeed it cannot be mistaken.

Bernard in his sermons dwells on "the kiss of his mouth" (Song 1.2) for which the soul yearns. It is not "a meeting of lips ... but a full infusion of joys, a revelation of secrets, a wonderful and inseparable mingling of the light from above and the mind on which it is shed." The soul "loves most chastely ... in purity of spirit," yet "ardently." In seeking God's kiss the soul "calls on the Holy Spirit, through whom she will receive at the same time both the taste of knowledge and the savor of grace."[14]

The soul, the Bride, is not always with the Bridegroom, and when he is gone she longs for his return. The interrupted presence of God is what Bernard experienced in his own contemplative life, and in one sermon he speaks of his own experience. "I tell you," he says, "that the Word has come even to me— I speak in my foolishness—and that he has come more than once." Bernard's confession of "foolishness" refers to St. Paul's asking the Corinthians to "bear with me in a little foolishness" (2 Cor. 11.1). Bernard, however, is as confident as Paul when he speaks of his experience of God. He does not know "the moment of his coming" or "where he comes from when he enters my soul, or where he goes when he leaves it," although he is aware that "he does not come from within me," for the "Word is far, far above." He knows when the Word is present in his soul, for "he moves and soothes and pierces my heart." He "begins to root up ... set what was cold on fire." By the "warmth of my heart ... did I know he was there." "My faults were purged and my body's yearnings brought under control" and "my secret faults were revealed." But the Word is not always with Bernard. "When "the Word has

---

12   St. Bernard of Clairvaux, Sermon 84 on the Song of Songs, in *Bernard of Clairvaux: Selected Works*, p. 274.

13   St. Bernard of Clairvaux, Sermon 7 on the Song of Songs, in *Bernard of Clairvaux: Selected Works*, p. 231.

14   St. Bernard of Clairvaux, Sermons 2, 7, and 8 on the Song of Songs, in *Bernard of Clairvaux: Selected Works*, pp. 216, 232, and 239.

left me," he says, "and all these things become dim and weak and cold ... I know that he has gone." As often as he departs, Bernard exclaims, "so often will I seek him ... with a burning desire of the heart."[15] Though Bernard is here describing his own experience, he is aware that it is not his soul alone that is the Bride. He uses "brides" in the plural in a sermon in which he urges others to believe "so that by their faith they may in the future have the reward of experience."[16]

Experiences and Biblical Images of God's Love

Bernard presents us with an image of God's love that helps us understand God's love through that image. God's love for individual souls is like a Bridegroom's love for his Bride, full of joy and the fervor of "the kiss of his mouth." In this image, God's love is *experienced*, though it is not constantly felt. Bernard helps to provide an understanding of God's love by providing a description of that experience. In Bernard's ecstatic and relatively brief experiences of God's love, in God's kiss, there is an infusion of joy and revelation. Bernard's experience is that of a contemplative. Others in Bernard's Christian tradition, and in the Judaic and Islamic traditions, can speak of other experiences of God's love.

Many in the theistic traditions may have a sense of God's presence. The Psalms richly express this sense. The Psalmist finds God "robed in majesty" in all his creation (Ps. 93.1). God's presence is in the "heavens [which are] telling the glory of God," though without speech or words (Ps. 19. 1–3), as it is found in all of life, even in life's everyday aspects. For the Psalmist God keeps even our "going out" and our "coming in" (Ps. 121.8). And the Psalmist experiences God's pervasive love as his "steadfast love," which is "before my eyes" (Ps. 26.3).

---

15   St. Bernard of Clairvaux, Sermon 74 on the Song of Songs, in *Bernard of Clairvaux: Selected Works*, pp. 254–56.

16   St. Bernard of Clairvaux, Sermon 84 on the Song of Songs, in *Bernard of Clairvaux: Selected Works*, p. 277.

Commonly among believers there may be a sense of the "fear of God," awe and reverence before God, and a sense of joy—the religious joy Bernard found in his experience—expressed in their rejoicing and thankfulness. Especially joy, but also rejoicing, and thankfulness may be within or in response to a believer's felt sense of God's love. In a previous chapter we noted how believers' thanking God may be visible to nonbelievers as a sign of believers' love of God. Now we see that their thanking God and rejoicing in God may also express their sense of God's love. In general when God is felt as supportive or as answering a deeply felt need his love is experienced on analogy with the love one person gives to another in human relationships. In this way there may be a felt sense of God's love in times of trial or even despair.

In the Bible there are various images of God that represent to believers God's love. There is the image of God as the Good Shepherd, who lovingly cares for his flock (Is. 40.11, Ps. 23.1, and Mt. 10.14). A primary image of God is as a father, our Everlasting and Heavenly Father (Is. 9.6 and Mt. 6.9). With this image God's love is presented as like a parent's protective and supportive love, and so it may be experienced. In a very different image, God

> will cover you with his pinions,
> and under his wings you will find
> refuge. (Ps. 91.4)

Here the image is of a loving mother protecting her fledglings. These images express what God's love is like, and to an extent what God is like, as does the image of the Bridegroom, although as images all of these representations of God are metaphorical.

Julian of Norwich

Julian of Norwich, the fourteenth-century English anchorite, referred to God as Mother. She was not the first in the Christian tradition to find a maternal character to God's love, and in fact a maternal characterization of God's comforting and protective love is to be found in the Bible, as in Psalm 19, as was just noted.[17] In the *Showings* Julian says, "Jesus Christ, who opposes good to evil, is our true Mother. We have our being from him where the foundation of motherhood begins." However, Julian develops the image of God as Mother and God's maternal love in her own distinctive way. Part of what makes Julian's treatment of the Motherhood of God image and theme distinctive is her application of it to the Trinity. In the chapter of the *Showings* just quoted she goes on to say,

> Our great Father, almighty God, who is being, knows us and loved us before time began. Out of this knowledge, in his most wonderful deep love, by the prescient eternal counsel of all the blessed Trinity, he wanted the second person to become our Mother, our brother and our saviour. From this it follows that as truly as God is our Father, so truly is God our Mother.[18]

Yet what is most distinctive and revealing in Julian's use of the theme of God's maternal love is the concrete imagery she uses to body forth that love. Important in her understanding of God's love is that whatever we do we cannot alienate that love. She says in reference to the love of "Mother Jesus,"

> For we shall truly see in heaven without end that we have sinned grievously in this life; and notwithstanding this, we shall truly see that we were never hurt in his love, nor were we ever of less value in his sight.[19]

---

17   Jean Leclercq, O.S.B. In his Preface to *Julian of Norwich: Showings* cites various earlier Christian authors who use maternal imagery, and as well biblical passages; he notes that the theme of God as Mother is also found in other religious traditions, particularly Hinduism. *Julian of Norwich: Showings*, trans. Edmund Colledge, O.S.A (New York; Ramsey, NJ; and Toronto; Paulist Press, 1978), pp. 9 and 10.

18   Julian of Norwich, *Showings*, Long Text, chap. 59, in *Julian of Norwich: Showings*, pp. 295 and 296.

19   Julian of Norwich, *Showings*, Long Text, chap. 61, in *Julian of Norwich: Showings*, p. 300.

Traditionally in Christianity God's love is not withdrawn from us in our failings. What Julian highlights is that as a mother loves her wayward children without lessening their value so God's motherly love does not lessen with human misdeeds.

How the love of Mother Jesus is to be sought as maternal love Julian communicates concretely in the following:

> often when our falling and wretchedness are shown to us, we are so much afraid and so greatly ashamed of ourselves that we scarcely know where we can put ourselves. But then our courteous Mother does not wish us to flee away, for nothing would be less pleasing to him; but he then wants us to behave like a child. For when it is distressed and frightened, it runs quickly to its mother; and if it can do no more, it calls to the mother for help with all its might. So he wants us to act as a meek child, saying: My kind Mother, my gracious Mother, my beloved Mother, have mercy on me. I have made myself filthy and unlike you, and I may not and cannot make it right except with your help and grace.[20]

In order for God's love to be understood and felt as comforting or supportive or to be found in human experience it must in some way be grasped in human understanding. The image of God as Mother and the other images of God and his love provide that understanding. If Aquinas is right, we can understand that God's love is analogous to human love. At the same time, according to another religious intuition God's love as infinite love is beyond human understanding. There are two religious sensibilities here. For one God's eminent and infinite love is to be understood or partially understood using images of human love, and in this way the infinite endpoint of the asymptote of love is approached in understanding. For the other God's love is the infinite endpoint of the asymptote of human love that by its nature is beyond human

---

20   Julian of Norwich, *Showings*, Long Text, chap. 61, in *Julian of Norwich: Showings*, p. 301.

understanding. In this way God's love is made understandable and accessible to human experience by the image of a mother's love, or a bridegroom's love for one sensibility, and at the same time it remains at its uttermost beyond human understanding for the other sensibility. These two religious sensibilities and their theological correlates—that followed by St. Thomas Aquinas, which allows a human understanding of God's love, and the apophatic theology of Dionysius, which puts God's love beyond conception and understanding—exist together as complements. This complementarity is not unique to Christianity.

Both sensibilities are found in Judaism, of which the mysticism of Kabbalah is a part. In Kabbalah the highest and first *sefirah* or emanation is *Keter* or Crown, which is coeternal with *Ein Sof*, the ultimate reality of God beyond contemplation and articulation. In medieval Kabbalah there are emanating from *Keter* nine *sefirot* (plural of *sefirah*), including *Binah* (Understanding), *Hokhmah* (Wisdom), *Hesed* (Love), and *Hod* (Majesty). *Ein Sof* is in accord with the sensibility that God is beyond comprehension and attribution, whereas the lower *sefirot*, representing the attributes of God, accord with the sensibility that God's nature and attributes can be approached in understanding.[21]

In the Hindu tradition again there are two parallel complementary religious sensibilities. For one Hindu sensibility the highest reality, Brahman, is beyond description and attribution (*nirguna*), and for the other Brahman is merciful, generous, compassionate, and more (*saguna*).[22] In the Christian tradition the depth of God's love and many of its ways are a mystery, and this is in accord with the apophatic tradition. If God's love is always present, then it is with us in the time of loss and grief, and it is present in the ravages of war and in the suffering from disease and natural disasters

---

21   Daniel Chanan Matt, Introduction to *Zohar: The Book of Enlightenment* (New York; Ramsey, NJ; and Toronto: Paulist Press, 1983), pp. 33-5.

22   Vasudha Narayanan, "The Hindu Tradition," in *World Religions: Eastern Traditions*, 2nd ed., ed. Willard G. Oxtoby (Oxford. UK and New York: Oxford University Press, 2002), p. 79.

that has seemed to many to contradict the goodness of God and his love. Such reflections, along with the desire not to in any way limit God, lead those in the apophatic tradition to say that God's love and its ways are ineffable in their mystery. Yet religiously God's love can be modeled by different images and experienced in their terms, or experienced as the Psalmist experienced it, as pervasive as God's presence. Finally the apophatic tradition and the contrasting tradition represented by St. Thomas Aquinas, St. Bernard of Clairvaux, and Julian of Norwich, as well as the two contrasting religious sensibilities that we identified, complement one another in the broad Christian tradition, as their counterpart sensibilities complement one another in other traditions.

V. BUDDHIST AND HINDU TRADITIONS

IN THE EASTERN NONTHEISTIC TRADITIONS there is no place in religious sensibility for God's love. Unlike the worldviews of the Western theistic traditions, the Eastern nontheistic traditions do not see God as the supreme reality of the universe. Although in Buddhism minor gods are recognized, and in Vajrayāna Buddhism a wide range of deities have various functions, such gods are not comparable to God as conceived in the Western Abrahamic traditions. However, in Hinduism's theistic tradition there is a place for the love of Krishna or another god and that god's love, while in forms of Buddhism there is a place for heavenly compassion.

In Mahāyāna Buddhism there are *bodhisattvas*, those who come to the edge of *nirvāna* but hold back out of compassion for those in the world. Distinct from celestial *buddhas* they abide in a heavenly realm and receive petitionary prayers. A principal *bodhisattva*, Avalokiteśvara, is particularly associated with compassion. The cosmic compassion of this *bodhisattva* and that of other venerated *bodhisattvas* may be compared to God's love in Western traditions.

Another devotional form of Buddhism is Jōdo, or Amida Buddhism, in which the celestial *buddha*, Amida Buddha, is venerated and relied on in the quest for salvation and Buddhahood. Amida Buddha is the object of devotion and it is through his compassion that the Buddhist believer in Amida Buddha hopes for salvation.[23]

In Hinduism, similarly, contrasting with its advaistist, or nondualistic, form there is the *bhakti mārga*, or way of devotion, in which worshipful devotion may be given to Rāma or Krishna, or to another deity. In strains of theistic Hinduism that are devoted to Krishna, the goddess Radha may be seen as the female complement to the male Krishna, so that the two are worshiped together. Also Radha may be seen as an ideal of *bhakti* worship of Krishna.[24] Her image of goddess merges with the devotee, and she and Krishna are worshipped in their love relationship.

Between the sixth and ninth centuries, in the early period of the heritage, the Alvars of South India wrote poems of devotion to lord Vishnu. The Alvars were both poets and saints who wrote their poems or hymns in the vernacular (Tamil). One of the twelve traditionally recognized Alvars was Nammalvar, many of whose poems express love for Vishnu. Thus in one we find,

> Our Kannan dark as rain cloud
> has stolen my heart
> and it has gone away with him
>   all by itself.

Kannan is Tamil for Krishna, the Dark One, who is an avatar, or incarnation, of Vishnu. Nammalvar's poems also express Vishnu's love for his beloved. In an amorous exchange that may be compared to the Song of Songs the loving lord Vishnu speaks of his beloved as follows:

> her eyes
> bring enough to buy a world
> eyes,
> each large as the palm of a hand

---

23   Roy C. Amore and Julia Ching, "The Buddhist Tradition," in *World Religions: Eastern Traditions*, 2nd ed., ed. Willard G. Oxtoby (Oxford, UK and New York: Oxford University Press, 2002), pp. 204–5.

24   Narayanan, "The Hindu Tradition," pp. 64 and 100.

shaped like a carp,
dropping pearls
and grief yellow as gold.

And the beloved replies,

Skin dark as young mango leaf
    is wilting.
Yellow patches spread all over me.
Night is as long as several lives.

In another poem or hymn we have,

singing himself
becoming for my sake
honey milk sugarcane
    ambrosia
becoming the lord of gardens too
    he stands there
consuming me.

In these poems there are other voices and other themes, such as that of inflation, as when the beloved, possessed by her lover, takes on his attributes. Her mother (one of the other voices) says this in one poem,

"I made the world
    surrounded by the sea," says she,
"I became the world
    surrounded by the sea," says she.[25]

What is to be noted, however, is how Nammalvar uses the image of sensual love to express the love of Vishnu for his beloved. Given the cultural distance

---

25   These poems are in A. K. Ramanujan's translation from Tamil, in *Hymns for the Drowning: Poems for Vishnu by Nammalvar*, trans. A. K. Ramanujan (Princeton, NJ: Princeton University Press, 1981), pp. 34, 62, 63, 70, and 77. Nammalvar is known by several other names, including Maran, Catakopan, and Sathakopa.

between them, his image may surprise us in its closeness to St. Bernard's image of the Bride and Bridegroom and the sensual love imagery of the Song of Songs.

In our human effort to grasp in some way God's love, our images are constantly and of necessity those of human love, love for another or others. God's love, in the language of St. Thomas Aquinas, is that love more eminently. It is the endpoint of the asymptote of that love.

Chapter Eight

The Circle of Love

I. INTRODUCTION

THE CIRCLE OF LOVE encloses all that uttermost love—or a religious love that begins to approach uttermost love as an ideal of love—will love. It is the circle of the horizon of love, and as the visual horizon of a viewer changes and encompasses more as she or he advances toward it, so the horizon of love and that which we can see to be within the circle may change with an advance toward the perimeter of the horizon.

What will the expanded perimeter of the circle of love encompass? What is the scope of uttermost love or the religious love that begins to approach it? Or, as we asked at the end of chapter 2, What will it love? For Judaism, Christianity, and Islam the circle of love explicitly includes God, and from the Christian and Jewish perspectives, and from other religious perspectives as well, it clearly includes one's neighbors, understood as all other human beings. But some have raised doubts about whether such universal love of neighbor is realistically or psychologically possible. Their doubts do not stem from the human ability, or inability, to control and come to have feelings of love, but arise from reflection on the human capacity, or incapacity, to have love for those who are distant and beyond our ken or acquaintance. In this way a doubt is raised about a form of love that has seemed to many to be very clearly included in the circle of uttermost love. We will examine this doubt and address it in section II.

Though a traditional Christian or Jewish understanding might limit the compass of uttermost love and religious love that begins to approach it to love of God and love of neighbor, in the centuries of the modern era religious sensibilities have developed that see the embrace of religious love as having a wider scope. These sensibilities bring us to a question that is central to this chapter: What created beings besides human beings will the circle of love encompass? In pursuing this question, as we will do in section III, we will heed several voices. Not all of these speak from within a defined religious perspective, but many that we will heed do. As we will see, in the modern era several have sought to widen the Christian understanding of the circle of love.

In section IV, we will turn to the other form of love that is widely recognized by Jews, Christians, and Muslims as included in the circle of religious love: love of God. In this section we will consider what place there can be for either explicit or implicit love of God in nontheistic religious traditions.

II. A PERCEIVED PROBLEM WITH LOVE OF STRANGERS WHO ARE DISTANT

THE NEIGHBOR that the Good Samaritan finds in need is a stranger to him, but not a distant stranger. Many of those who are our neighbors are distant from us, perhaps half a world away. Most we have never seen and never will see. The Samaritan when he sees the need of the man set upon by robbers is moved by compassion. But, it has been asked, how can we be expected to be moved by compassion for those we do not know and cannot see, those who are distant strangers?

Adam Smith (1723–90) in *The Theory of Moral Sentiments* asked his readers to suppose that the "great empire of China ... was suddenly swallowed up by an earthquake." How, he asked, would a European be affected by news of this calamity? He would be little disturbed, was Adam Smith's reply. He would feel a greater "disturbance," Smith judged, "if he was to lose his little finger to-morrow" than by "the ruin of a hundred millions of his brethren." Such are our "passive feelings." At the same time, he allowed, the "generous" always and the "mean" often "sacrifice their own interests to the greater interests of others" acting out of "conscience," not for the love of neighbor or mankind, but for "the love of what is honorable and noble [and for the] superiority of [their] own characters."[1]

Smith's rumination on how a European might care more about losing his little finger than about millions of Chinese dying may be compared to David Hume's reflection in the *Treatise*, noted in chapter 2, that preferring the destruction of the world to scratching one's little finger is not "contrary to reason."[2] For Hume it would not be contrary to reason to never have the "passion" of love for another. For Smith we do sometimes, even often, sacrifice our self-interest for others, but not out of love for others, and we are never more "disturbed" (moved) by the suffering of others than by our own personal discomfort, especially—in the light of his example—when those subjected to suffering are distant.

The contemporary author Carlo Ginzburg pursues a line of reflection on human moral psychology similar to that of Adam Smith. Ginzburg reflects on the waning or extinction of compassion specifically caused by distance. He says that "distance, if pushed to an extreme, can generate a total lack of compassion for our fellow humans," which at least allows that we are capable of having compassion for those who are not distant. But, he suggests, a Parisian would feel, can feel, no compassion for a contemporary Chinese Mandarin who has been killed. He reflects also on the distance of killing from afar in aerial bombing or in the use of missiles (and we can add drones). Although sometimes remorse may be felt, such distance can make killing easier, Ginzburg observes. It can blunt or extinguish compassion and even concern, although there are exceptions. Ginzburg cites the remorse felt by Claude Eatherly, a pilot who had a supportive role in the bombing mission that dropped the atomic bomb on Hiroshima. Something similar to the effect of physical distance

---

1   Adam Smith, *The Theory of Moral Sentiments*, 6th ed., ed. Knud Haakonssen (Cambridge, UK: Cambridge University Press, 2002), chap. III, section 4, pp. 157–58. *The Theory of Moral Sentiments* was originally published in 1759, and between 1761 and 1790 went through six editions, some significantly revised.

2   David Hume's *A Treatise of Human Nature* was published twenty years before Adam Smith's *The Theory of Moral Sentiments*.

applies to a sense of psychological distance. However, Ginzburg notes,"[n]ormal German citizens who were turned into mass murderers," as members of a German reserve police battalion that participated in the killing of Jews in Poland in the Nazi era, "were slightly disturbed by the perspective of doing their usual job when by chance they came across Jews they had known in the past." If not a feeling of compassion, at least moral doubt surfaced when their usual psychological distance was destroyed by recognition.[3]

Ginzburg and Smith capture a psychological truth about a human propensity not to have empathy, sympathy, love, or compassion for those who are distant from us or over our emotional horizon. Yet, as the exceptions Ginzburg cites suggest, we have other psychological proclivities that are just as significant. Agencies that seek support for the deprived of the world may present their appeals with pictures of children or adults in obvious physical need. Such pictures can serve to awaken a sympathetic response and move us to compassion and *agapeistic* love. They do, some may say, because they manipulate our feelings. This may be so. But let us observe the significance of the possibility of such manipulation. It can only be effective if we have the potential of such feelings, rather as the Dalai Lama suggests when he expresses his conviction that human beings are "loving by nature" and "disposed toward love and compassion."[4] Moreover, in many instances in today's world, at least brief feelings of compassion for distant strangers can be awakened without manipulation. When Adam Smith wrote in the eighteenth century, Europeans, as he says, might not be "disturbed" by distant disasters affecting distant strangers. In today's world of instant media coverage and social media reports of earthquakes and other natural disasters it is not uncommon for many, independently of appeals, freely and quickly to respond to the plight of those in need.

---

3   Carlo Ginzburg, "Killing a Chinese Mandarin: The Moral Implications of Distance," *Critical Inquiry*, vol. 21, no. 1 (Autumn 1994), pp. 56, 57, and 60. Regarding the reactions of members of the German reserve police battalion, Ginzburg cites Christopher R. Browning, *Ordinary Men: Reserve Police Battalion 101 and the Final Solution in Poland*.

4   His Holiness the Dalai Lama, *Ethics for a New Millennium* (New York: Riverhead Books, 1999), pp. 68 and 71.

St. Paul says that the requirements of God's law are written on our hearts. This means, as we saw in chapter 6, that the requirements of love are written on our hearts. Paul's claim entails that we have an interior sense of love's requirements. The Dalai Lama's claim is that we have a disposition or propensity to love and to have compassion. These are different claims, but we find in Paul's Christian tradition as well a perception of our capacity to love. In Jesus' parable of the Good Samaritan the Samaritan exhibits both the capacity and the propensity to have compassion, and when Jesus says to the one who has heard and responded to the parable, "Go and do likewise," his instruction implies that he too has the capacity and perhaps the suppressed propensity to have compassion.

It does not change matters if there is also a human disposition to be uncaring, selfish, or biased toward those we are not close to, propensities that are recognized in the Christian and Buddhist traditions. Nor does it change matters if we feel guilt in not responding. If we ought to have love and compassion and there are acts of compassion that we ought to perform, then guilt is the appropriate feeling if we fail in either affection or action. Thus, although Smith and Ginzburg may be right about the compassion-denying propensities they present, this does not deny that at the same time we can also have the opposite propensity or capacity to respond with love and compassion in our actions and, for one strain of religious sensibility, in our feelings.

Human Love as a Template for Religious Love

Within theistic belief God's love is the endpoint of the asymptote of love, but moreover, the asymptote of love is the asymptote of human love. Whatever understanding we have of God's love, following St. Thomas Aquinas, we gain from human love. At the same time God's love as uttermost love embodies the ideal of the love human beings are to have. This means that our understanding of both God's love and the ideal of the love we are to have for God and neighbors has its roots in human love. If this is true, then we might expect to find in some expressions of human love indications of what it is to love God or our neighbors. And arguably this seems to be the case. In chapter 6 we noted several ways, expressed in social actions, that God might be loved through loving others. Here, though, we should direct our attention to expressions of more intimate forms of human love that are more commonplace and familiar in human experience. No culture is without human love in an intimate form—romantic and marital love, a mother's love for her child, the binding love of friendship—and often such love has been memorialized in one or another artistic form. In the West, romantic love has figured in poetry, drama, fiction, and the visual arts. Different treatments have presented romantic love as tragic (as in Shakespeare's *Romeo and Juliet* and Giacomo Puccini's *La Bohème*) or as comic (as in Shakespeare's *Much Ado About Nothing*). It can be reduced to the philanderer's seduction (as in the various renderings of the legend of Don Juan) or elevated to supernatural passion (as in Richard Wagner's treatment of Siegfried and Brünnhilde's love). Also, though, romantic love has been given expression by poets as their own love for their beloved. One instance of this is in John Donne's poem titled simply "Song," addressed to his wife and written when he had to part from her for a time in 1612. Full of complex feelings, the poem communicates Donne's deep attachment to his wife, how they "keep" one another and in "sleep" will never be parted.

We find an expression of a wife's love for her husband in a poem by the Chinese poet Li Bai (or Li Po or Li Bo) written in the eighth century and translated by Ezra Pound. The poem, "The River Merchant's Wife: A Letter," is in the form of a letter written by a young sixteen-year-old wife to her husband, who has been away for almost half a year plying his trade as a merchant. In the poem—her letter—she does not announce her loneliness, but the depth and delicacy of her longing are evinced in the poem's lines. As the poem concludes she tells her husband that if he will send word of the way he will take coming home, she will go partway to meet him.

Though they are brief and subdued, in these two expressions of human love we find an expression of human feeling that can serve as a template for religious love of God in its aspect as *eros*. Donne's and Li Bai's (and Pound's) mode of expression is literary, but other expressions have been more popular. The lyrics of popular songs express the desire, longing, and commitment of romantic love."

Such lyrics, like poetry, can express the utter devotion and longing of romantic love and model the utter devotion and longing of religious love for God. The love we have in our most intense and intimate human relationships is in this way a template for our love for God. Paul said that God's law is written on our hearts, and one way for this to be so is that what love of God and of our neighbors requires is shown to us in our closest human love relationships. How better to begin to understand the longing for God than in terms of the longing for the beloved? How better to begin to understand utter devotion to God than in terms of the utter devotion given to the beloved? St. Bernard of Clairvaux understood God's love in terms of the Bridegroom's love for the Bride, as Nammalvar in the Hindu *bhakti* tradition understood God's love as Vishnu's love for his beloved, but, as they also understood, the same image turned around presents love *for* God. And at the same time how better to begin to understand the spontaneity of the love we are to have for God and the love to be given to our neighbors than in terms of the spontaneous affection we have for our children? As Bernard's image of the Bride's longing and love models human love for God, so Julian of Norwich's image of a Mother's love for her needful child models both God's love and the compassionate love we are to have for our neighbors in religious love's aspect as *agape*.

For St. Thomas Aquinas, as we saw in the preceding chapter, we can come to some understanding of God's love through an extrapolation from human love. Our human love, for Aquinas, can provide only a dim projection of God's love, to which it is "analogous," but human love is the source of our understanding of God's love. In a similar way, we now see, human love in its intimate forms may be the source of our understanding what it is to love God and to love our neighbors. It may be as C. S. Lewis said: "The human loves can be glorious images of Divine love," if we understand Divine love as *agapeistic* love of God or our neighbors.[5]

Love's Expressions in Different Relationships

Love's character in both its exterior and interior dimensions is significantly determined by the different relationships in which it is manifested. In chapter 2 we saw that *eros* and *agape* can be combined in religious love.

---

5   C. S. Lewis, *The Four Loves* (New York: Harcourt, Brace, and Company, 1960), p. 20. Lewis understands Divine love as what he calls "Gift-love," an *agapeistic* love that may be given by one person to other persons. *The Four Loves*, p. 11.

Religious love for God may take the form of *eros*, but religious love for God and others at its core is *agape* (or *caritas* or charity), a love that asks for nothing in return. As love of neighbor it may be manifested for those who are beyond one's immediate ken, but it may also be manifested in close relationships; and, though the nature of *agape* does not change, the expressions of religious love in distant and close relationships may be very different. Just as we may understand that, in the Christian tradition, the requirements of love are written on our hearts, so we may understand that the different expressions of love are shown to us in our different relationships to others.

We find in the Gospel accounts of Christ's life and death different expressions of his love. His dying on the cross was an expression of his love, but his submission to his crucifixion for the sake of others was an expression of universal love, not individual love. It contrasts in its affective dimension with his love for Mary and Martha and for their brother Lazarus. Jesus loves Lazarus, and Mary and Martha (Jn. 11.5), and though they believe in him as the Son of God and call him Lord, he loves them as one who knows them and is a friend. When their brother Lazarus dies Mary and Martha send for Jesus. We are told that on arriving at the house of Mary and Martha Jesus was "deeply moved in his spirit and troubled" when he saw Mary weeping for her brother's loss, and that Jesus too wept (Jn. 11. 33 and 35). Jesus expresses his love in a way appropriate in a close relationship. On the cross his love, though greater in being a universal love for all, does not have such a personal and individual expression. The Greek word used for love in love of neighbor is a form of *agape*, and the Greek word used for love when we are told that Jesus loved Mary and Martha and their brother Lazarus is also *agape*, or its verbal form. Jesus' love is unfailingly *agape*, but the expression of his *agapeistic* love varies.

Many in today's world may have little love or compassion for the stranger who is distant, as Smith and Ginzburg perceived; or they may have a sporadic concern when a crisis of famine or flood is in the news, which, as was argued, shows the potential for sympathy, compassion, and *agape*. When *agape* is present there necessarily is an affective dimension, but the affect of love can be influenced by geographical and psychological distance. Additionally, in general the closeness or distance of the relationship determines the form of affective response, whether it is personal and demonstrative or more distantly given, as is evident in Jesus' different expressions of *agapeistic* love. As we saw in chapter 3, even within the range of close *agapeistic* love relationships the expression of love can vary. The expression of *agapeistic* love for a spouse may be very different from the expression of *agapeistic* love for a friend; and the *agapeistic* love of a parent for one child may be different from that for a second child with different needs. Just as in chapter 2 we saw how *agape* is compatible with *eros*, in chapter 3 we indirectly saw that *agape* is compatible with and may be expressed in *philia* and *storge*. Also it may be expressed for distant strangers who are never seen, but to whose need there is a compassionate response. Such a response is *agapeistic*, but again its expression is determined by the relationship. The interior response of *agape*, when it is for distant strangers, may be of less emotional intensity than it would be in *agape* given to another that one is close to or to a stranger in need that one encounters face to face, as the Samaritan encountered the man set upon by robbers. This does not mean that the response to distant strangers is not *agape* compassionately given, only that *agape*'s expression, including its interior side, is significantly determined by the relationship in which it is given.

What we have just observed about relationships determining the expression of religious love or *agape* does not negate the religious perception that love of neighbor must be for all without distinction; otherwise it is the biased love of conventional morality. But this in turn does not mean that the *expression* of religious love is undifferentiated. Religious love for our neighbors is without distinction in being universally given to our neighbors and in being never slighted. It is differentiated in having different expressions in the different relationships in which it is manifested.

III. THE CIRCLE OF LOVE EXPANDED

IN THE PREVIOUS SECTION our concern was with the scope of love of neighbor, and with the varied expressions of that love in different human relationships. Traditionally within Judaism and Christianity religious love is the love commanded by the two great commandments to love God and one's neighbors.

In the modern era, however, different voices have raised the question whether the circle of love is or should be limited to God and our human neighbors and suggested that the circle be expanded.

Albert Schweitzer (1875–1965) may be remembered by most as a medical missionary who devoted more than half his life to providing medical aid to the West Africans of what would become Gabon, which he did from 1913 to 1965. Schweitzer was also a theologian and, beyond an active life of service to those in need that expressed his love of his neighbors, he urged the acceptance of a wider ethic that he called "Reverence for Life." One follows the ethic of Reverence for Life, for Schweitzer, "when life, as such, is sacred to him, that of plants and animals as that of his fellow men, and when he devotes himself helpfully to all life that is in need of help." "The ethic of Reverence for Life," he said, "is the ethic of love widened into universality," so that it applies to all life. It is for Schweitzer "the ethic of Jesus" traced to its "logical consequence." What proves the truth of a view of the world, he thought, is that it brings us into "a spiritual relation to life and the universe [that] makes us into inward men with an active ethic."[6] Such an active ethic was, in Schweitzer's life, expressed in service to humanity and respect for all life.

Schweitzer in effect expanded the circle of love as it had been traditionally understood in Christianity so that it would include all living beings. He was, he believed, changing Christianity as it had been understood without departing from "the ethic of Jesus." It seems clear that religions evolve and religious beliefs can change. John Hick observes that within Christianity, though the "words and symbols," such as *God, Christ, Cross,* and *Church,* have remained the same, Christian belief has changed over the centuries. As an example he points to a change in Christian religious and theological belief about the significance of the Cross, of Christ's death on the cross. For centuries it was viewed as a ransom (following Mk. 10.45). Then in the eleventh century St. Anselm argued for a "satisfaction" theory, according to which Jesus' death was a full satisfaction for the sins of the world. Today, though,

---

6   Albert Schweitzer, *Out of My Life and Thought: An Autobiography,* trans. C. T. Campion (New York: Henry Holt and Company, 1949), pp. 228, 232, and 158–59.

Hick suggests that neither of these views of "an atoning transaction to enable God to forgive sinners" prevails in Christian belief and "the death of Jesus has become for many Christians . . . the manifestation of a self-giving love which is an earthly reflection of the divine love."[7]

Another example mentioned by Hick is the Christian belief about God's creation.[8] A central and traditional Christian, Jewish, and Islamic belief is that God is the Creator of all that is. However, within Christianity the understanding of this belief has changed in the last 150 years or so. When Charles Darwin presented his evolutionary theory in 1859, it was widely thought that it contradicted the religious belief that God created human beings and other species, and indeed it does if the creation story in the first chapter of the book of Genesis is read literally. It does because Darwin's account denies that all species were created at the same time about 6,000 years ago. If, though, the first chapter of Genesis is understood as not giving a literal step-by-step account of a six-day creation, while still telling of God's role as Creator, as many contemporary Christians understand it, the incompatibility disappears. Other examples could be cited. One that has more to do with religious practice is the change in belief about the Christian necessity of rejecting violence at the personal level and in the form of war. In the early centuries of the Common Era, the belief that their religion required the rejection of war was held by many Christians.[9] In succeeding centuries this conviction waned, so that today, sadly for some, this belief has changed. In short, religious beliefs, and Christian beliefs in particular, have changed over time, and we can understand Schweitzer's widening of the circle of love as just such a change.

There are, to be sure, questions about all the beings that are to be included in Schweitzer's widened circle of love. Are disease-causing protozoans, bacteria, and viruses to be included? (We will return to this question in chapter 10.) And

---

7   John Hick, *A Christian Theology of Religions: The Rainbow of Faiths* (Louisville, KY: Westminster John Knox Press, 1995), pp. 126 and 129–31.

8   Hick, *A Christian Theology of Religions*, p. 131.

9   C. John Cadoux, *The Early Christian Attitude to War* (New York: Seabury Press, 1982), p. 245. *The Early Christian Attitude to War* was originally published in 1919.

of course Schweitzer's widening of the circle of love will not become an established Christian belief until Christians widely accept it. This began to happen in the twentieth century as other Christian voices joined Schweitzer's. Onward from about the middle of the twentieth century, the theologian and seminary teacher Howard Thurman expressed in his thought and writings a sense of God's presence in all the earth. He expressed sympathy for the suggestion "that historical Christianity has misunderstood or misinterpreted the teaching of Jesus concerning the reverence for life," and reflecting on the "whole process of nature," his own body, and "a study of other forms of life" he said,

> I react to what I observe: this is the Hand of God fashioning His creation. Such a mood of reverence has a transfer value for me also. It moves me directly into the experience of what Schweitzer calls "reverence for life."[10]

In the twentieth century, which was a time of developing environmental concern, other Christian voices joined Schweitzer's and Thurman's. Another theologian, Sallie McFague, in a book that examines different models or images of God, treats images of God as Mother (*agape*), Lover *(eros)*, and Friend (*philia*), but also the image of the world as "God's body." The Gospel of John, she points out, says, "God so loved the *world*" (Jn. 3.16; McFague's emphasis). She goes on to say,

> if we understand God's saving presence as directed to the fulfilment of all of creation—with each of us part of that whole—we participate in God's love not as individuals but as members of an organic whole, God's body.

Conceiving of the world as God's body we can conceive of God being present to it as "mother, lover, and friend of the last and least of all creation."[11]

---

10   Howard Thurman, *Disciplines of the Spirit* (New York; Evanston, IL; and London: Harper & Row, 1963), pp. 67 and 92.

11   Sallie McFague, *Models of God: Theology for an Ecological, Nuclear Age* (Philadelphia, PA: Fortress Press, 1987), pp. 86 and 87.

In addition to individual voices, churches and church groups have issued statements of collective religious sentiment that reflect a new awareness of responsibility for the nonhuman beings of the earth. McFague's book was published in 1987. In 1989 the American Baptists issued a *Policy Statement on Ecology*, which said in part,

> The best understanding of the Biblical attitude of humanity's relationship with the Creation can be gained by a study of the Greek works which are the foundation of the New Testament.... The Greek word which is commonly translated "stewardship" [*oikonomos*] is the root word for economics and ecology. The literal translation of steward is manager of the household. As such, we are called to be managers of God's household, the earth and all that is in it.[12]

In a more recent document, *God's Earth Is Sacred: An Open Letter to Church and Society in the United States*, from the National Council of Churches, we find, "We believe that the Holy Spirit, who animates all creation, breathes in us and can empower us to participate in working toward the flourishing of Earth's community of life."[13] Pope John Paul II stated in his 1990 World Day of Peace message that

> Christians, in particular, realize that their responsibility within creation and their duty towards nature and the Creator are an essential part of their faith.... I should like to address directly my brothers and sisters in the Catholic Church, in order to remind them of their serious obligation to care for all creation.[14]

---

12   Available online, 2017, at http://www.abc-usa.org/wp-content/uploads/2012/06/3cology.pdf.

13   Available online, 2017, at http://www.ncccusa.org/news/14.02.05theological-statement.htm.

14   Pope John Paul II, *The Ecological Crisis: A Common Responsibility*. Quoted by Walter E. Grazer, "Strategy for Environmental Engagement: Building a Catholic Constituency," in *Christianity and Ecology: Seeking the Well-Being of Earth and Humans*, ed. Dieter T.

Similarly, Pope Francis in his homily during a mass that marked his inauguration in 2013 appealed to all to be "protectors of creation ... protectors of one another and of the environment." While these various statements are concerned with Christian responsibility and obligation, to the extent that their focus is on an obligation to *care* for the nonhuman beings in creation they evince the sense that the circle of love is to be expanded. And though the religious sensibility of a widened circle of love that is expanded by these Christian voices may not be accepted by many Christians, it nevertheless is a viable religious sensibility.

WITHIN CHRISTIAN THINKING AND SENSIBILITY there are to be found three possible models or images of the relationship that human beings have to the world of their environment. Each is given a succinct statement in the first two chapters of the book of Genesis.

The Dominion Model

The biblical origin and foundation for the dominion model are found in the first chapter of Genesis. After creating the firmament and the creatures of the earth, God says, "Let us make man in our image, after our likeness, and let them have dominion over the fish of the sea, and over the birds of the air, and over the cattle, and over all the earth, and over every creeping thing that creeps upon the earth" (Gen. 1.26). As St. Thomas Aquinas understood the idea of human dominion, it is that God has given plants and animals to humans for their use, and Aquinas quotes St. Augustine approvingly that "their life and death [that of plants and animals] is subject to our use by a very just ordination of the Creator."[15]

Hessel and Rosemary Radford Ruether (Cambridge, MA: Harvard University Press, 2000), p. 579.

15   St. Thomas Aquinas, *Summa Theologica* II-II, q. 64, a 1, in *St Thomas Aquinas, Summa Theologiae*, vol. 38, trans. Marcus Lefébure, O.P. (Cambridge, UK: Blackfriars in conjunction with McGraw-Hill, New York and Eyre & Spotiswoode, London, 1975), p. 21; and St. Augustine, *The City of God*, trans. Marcus Dods (New York: Modern Library,

There are different constructions of the dominion view, and not all are as extreme as that suggested by Aquinas and Augustine. The American Baptist *Policy Statement on Ecology*, for instance, says, "If we image God we will reflect in our dominion the love and the care that God has for the whole creation. . . ." For the dominion model, especially but not only in its strong form, God has given humans power over all creation, and humans are related to animals and "all the earth" as those with power are related to those over whom they have power. For the dominion model the power relationship that humankind has to the environment carries no moral responsibilities or obligations for humans toward the environment, and it recognizes no rights of natural beings. The natural beings of the earth have only instrumental value. While those who follow the dominion model may also "love and care" for the natural beings of creation in accord with the American Baptist *Policy Statement*, the dominion model does not require this. The dominion model, particularly in its strong version, has long played a background but justificatory role for the exploitation of animal populations, forests and grasslands, and the mineral resources of the earth.

The Stewardship Model

On this model human beings are stewards or keepers of the earth, which has been entrusted to them, that they may tend it and care for it. The origin of the stewardship model is also found in the book of Genesis. In the second chapter we read, "The Lord God took the man and put him in the garden of Eden to till it and keep it" (Gen. 2.15). It is the stewardship model that figures prominently in the American Baptists' *Policy Statement on Ecology*, and the stewardship verse is cited in the National Council of Churches' *Open Letter*.

Often stewardship is seen as a special form of dominion, or as dominion properly understood. The Anglican Bishop Hugh Montefiore has written, "Men hold their dominion over all nature as stewards and trustees for God."

1950), bk. I, 20, p. 26. Dods' translation is worded slightly differently from that used by Aquinas, although the sense is the same.

He continues, "They are confronted by an inalienable duty towards and concern for their total environment, present and future; and this duty towards environment does not merely include their fellow-men, but all nature and all life."[16] Like the dominion model, the stewardship model also postulates a central and informing relationship. For the stewardship model, the central relationship encompasses the environment but is essentially between humans and God. It is this relationship that determines what our human responsibility toward the environment is. In this relationship humans have been entrusted with God's property, and while humans are responsible for the environment, which is God's property, their responsibility is *to* God as the "owner" of the property entrusted to their stewardship. In this kind of relationship the obligations of stewardship—and how the property entrusted is to be treated—are importantly determined by the wishes and attitudes of the owner or God, and in the stewardship model God's desire is that those entrusted with keeping the earth should have concern for it and care for it.

In recent years, as we have seen, there is a religious and theological movement within Christianity toward stewardship, and away from a strong form of the dominion model, as evidenced by the American Baptists' *Policy Statement on Ecology* and the National Council of Churches' *Open Letter*.

The Goodness of Creation Model

The goodness of creation model, unlike the stewardship model, finds a basis for our obligation to care for the environment in the very goodness and worth of God's creation, which God found in it, or gave to it through his act of creation.

This model is also found in Genesis, in the early verses of the first chapter before the mention of human dominion over the earth. In these verses of Genesis we are told that God created the light, the dry land and the seas, the vegetation of the earth, and the living creatures and beasts of the earth, and, we are told, God saw that they were good (Gen. 1.10–25). As we might

---

16   Hugh Montefiore, *Can Man Survive?* (London: Fontana, 1970), p. 55.

expect, this model is also represented in church and theological literature. So it is that we find in the American Baptists' *Policy Statement on Ecology* the claim that "God made a world that is good in reality and potential," and in the National Council of Churches' *Open Letter* we find, "We believe that the Earth is home for all and that it has been created intrinsically good," with a reference to Genesis 1. It is the goodness of creation model that justifies the claim that we ought to take care of the earth *for its own sake*.

Summing up these three biblical models, for the dominion model God has given human beings the earth and all that is in it to do with as they will. For the stewardship model God has entrusted human beings with the earth, and they are charged by God to care for it. For the goodness of creation model all that God created is good, and human beings owe it to both God and the beings of the earth to respect and care for the beings of the earth.

Often, as we have seen, all three models, or pairs of them, are presented together and merge in Christian thinking. Howard Thurman quotes Psalm 8 in the King James Version, in which the Psalmist considers "thy heavens, the work of thy fingers" and reflects that God has made man "a little lower than the angels." And in Psalm 8, in what Thurman quotes, the Psalmist also reflects, "Thou madest him to have dominion over the works of thy hands; thou hast put all things under his feet," which is the dominion image of the human relationship to the earth. Nevertheless Thurman within a paragraph speaks of being moved "directly into the experience of what Schweitzer calls 'reverence for life.'"[17] In the National Council of Churches' *Open Letter*, though there is a clear rejection of the dominion model as a "false gospel" that proclaims "that our human calling is to exploit [the] Earth for our own ends alone," both the stewardship and goodness of creation models are put forward.

Notwithstanding that there is at times an ambivalence between the stewardship model and the goodness of creation model, and sometimes an embrace of the dominion model mitigated to allow caring for the earth, we see what seems to be a growing consensus in modern Christian thinking, at least among

---

17   Thurman, *Disciplines of the Spirit*, pp. 91–92.

some, that expands the circle of care and love to include nonhuman species. For some in this movement of consciousness the circle is expanded to include only other sentient, animal species. But for Schweitzer, plants, as living beings, are included in the circle, as is explicit in the goodness of creation model.

The widening of the circle of love in the consciousness of some Christians goes beyond sentient beings and living plants. Genesis tells us that all of creation is good. McFague, in quoting the Gospel of John, emphasizes that God's love is for the *world*. At about the midpoint of the twentieth century, Aldo Leopold proposed the idea of a "land ethic," in which human responsibility for soils, mountains, deserts, marshlands, and other nonliving natural beings of the earth was recognized. Unlike Schweitzer, Leopold, who was a forester and conservationist, did not speak as one seeking to enlarge the circle of love religiously understood, although he did speak of an "extension of ethics."[18] In the National Council of Churches' *Open Letter* the "protection of soils, air, and water" is recognized, for the sake of "ecological integrity" and "human environmental rights." Though Leopold's emphasis was on the integrity of natural beings, his vision did not rule out the judicious use of the land; yet he also said that it "is inconceivable to me that an ethical relation to land can exist without love, respect, and admiration for land, and a high regard for its value." He did not mean its instrumental or economic value but its intrinsic value.[19] In loving her or his neighbors, in the understanding of many who are religious, a person respects and responds to human neighbors in their intrinsic worth, which they have as much as she or he does. The religious sensibility reflected in this understanding affirms the inherent worth of those God loves in accord with the New Testament passage in which Jesus says that not even a sparrow "will fall to the ground without your Father's will," and "Fear not therefore; you are of more value than many sparrows" (Mt. 10. 29–31). In an analogous way, in a widened circle of love, in loving and caring for the living

18   Aldo Leopold, *The Land Ethic*, in *A Sand County Almanac*, enlarged edition (New York: Oxford University Press, 1966), pp. 217–41.

19   Leopold, *The Land Ethic*, p. 239.

and natural beings of the earth a person respects and responds to them in their integrity and intrinsic worth.

Some Christian thinkers have sought to attend to Leopold's vision of a land ethic.[20] They are at the moving edge of what for some is an evolving consciousness of the circle of Christian love, and it may be too early to say if Christian belief generally will change to embrace love for all of God's creation. However it is not too early to identify a widening sense of responsibility in our world for the resources and beings of the earth and, within Christian consciousness, a developing sense, among some, that the circle of love includes many beings in the world besides our human neighbors.

The change in consciousness that widens the circle of love requires a change in our ability to see. In order to have reverence for life in Schweitzer's sense, one needs to see the living things of the earth in a new way. And in order to care for the nonliving beings of the earth one needs to see them too in a new way. For that matter, in order to see the distant stranger as a neighbor one needs to see him or her in a new way. In Samuel Taylor Coleridge's "The Rime of the Ancient Mariner," the Mariner, alone on a ship adrift, in his despair looks upon the creatures of the sea as "slimy things." Then with a change in perception he sees them as "happy living things" and as beautiful beyond words. At that moment he can love them and bless them.[21] This change in the ability to see others is a change in heart in the sense that is important in religion. Being moved to love the stranger is to see the stranger in a new way, as loving the beings of the earth is to see them in a new way.

Here, to be sure, we find again the issue of our ability to control our feelings of love. As we saw in chapter 5, religious perspectives are divided on this issue. They can nevertheless agree that a change in feeling correlates so closely with a change in perception that they are indistinguishable, so that they are two aspects of the same change in consciousness.

---

20   See Daniel Cowdin, "The Moral Status of Otherkind in Christian Ethics," in *Christianity and Ecology*, pp. 261–90.

21   Samuel Taylor Coleridge, "The Rime of the Ancient Mariner," ll, 238 and 282–85.

IV. LOVE OF GOD

INCLUDED IN THE CIRCLE OF LOVE for the theistic traditions of Judaism, Christianity, and Islam is the love of God. In fact for these traditions the love of God may be paramount. Does this mean that for those in nontheistic traditions the circle of love cannot be complete? Or, to ask a slightly different question, does this mean that those in nontheistic traditions must be seen by those in theistic traditions as having an incomplete circle of love?

We have seen enough to understand that a negative answer should be given to both questions. Those in nontheistic traditions may yet love God implicitly through loving others compassionately. And those within theistic traditions, if they share the religious sensibility we first identified in chapter 3, can see others as loving God through loving others. In fact theistic believers may see themselves as explicitly loving God through loving others as we saw in chapter 6. A chief means of loving God is through loving others, and such love of God may be either implicit or explicit. Thus, though love of God is explicitly within the circle of love for Jews, Christians, and Muslims, that love of God may be implicit, and so not necessitate belief in God.

Must the circle of love include love of God in at least its implicit form? For theistic believers the answer to this question may be a resolute affirmative. The fact that Jews, Christians, and Muslims think of God differently—have different filled-out concepts of God—does not affect the case: in each of these traditions God is loved. Moreover, if we construe theistic belief broadly, we can recognize a love of God as love of Vishnu or Krishna in *bhakti* Hinduism and a close analogue in Jōdo or Amida Buddhism in the form of devotion to Amida Buddha. On the other hand, it must be recognized that attributing implicit love of God to Buddhists and Hindus presents many Buddhists and all nontheistic advaitist Hindus as loving a reality that they do not recognize—God. And this may be a compliment that they are not eager to accept. In their self-understanding there will be no place for love of God, either explicit or implicit. What there will be is a recognition and veneration of the Buddha or a recognition and reaching toward Brahman. While it may not be accurate to equate these profound religious attitudes with love, or with compassion, they can be seen to be like love of God in their required commitment and their life-orienting demands.

Chapter Nine

The Depth Of Love

I. INTRODUCTION

ALL LOVE has both an interior and an exterior dimension. Even trivial love has these two dimensions in some form. It is particularly significant that religious love as the love that begins to approach uttermost love has both dimensions. In considering the scope of religious love, as we did in the previous chapter, we were considering a question that relates primarily to the exterior dimension of religious love: What beings and kinds of beings will it embrace? In the previous chapter we presented the possibility of an expanded scope of religious love as it begins to approach uttermost love. The complement of the scope of religious love is its depth. Depth in love, gauged by commitment and affective response, relates primarily to the interior dimension of love. Giving without the requirement of return is a part of the interior dimension of all *agape*, and when this characteristic varies in its steadfastness from instance to instance of *agape*, such a variation is a variation in depth. Denial of self as a characteristic of love also relates primarily to the interior dimension of love. At the end of chapter 2, we asked what place denial of self would have in religious love that begins to approach uttermost love, and what form it would take. In section II we will address these questions.

The necessity of both an inner side and an exterior active side in religious love we have seen, and at this point that necessity may seem nearly self-evident. Some, though, have thought that religious love can be interior to the exclusion or near exclusion of an exterior expression. Such hyperinteriority will be the subject of section III of this chapter.

II. DEPTH OF RELIGIOUS LOVE

THE SCOPE OF RELIGIOUS LOVE, the circle of love, is comprised of all those beings that are objects of that love. The depth of religious love is the inner character of that love. The scope of love to a great extent correlates with its exterior dimension, and the depth of love to a great extent correlates with its interior dimension. The correlation is not perfect, though, for the depth of love is not wholly lodged in the feeling side of love. It is more its heartfelt character, expressed in both feeling and the action attendant upon feeling.

While all love has in some manner a feeling or interior side, not all love—not even all interpersonal love—has great depth. Love can be shallow. Even religious love can be shallow, and every instantiation of human religious love could have a greater depth. It is this sense that is expressed in the liturgical confession of sin in the words, "We have not loved you with our whole heart; we have not loved our neighbors as ourselves."[1] Religious love, many recognize, can deepen in many ways. Love that is given with a residual concern for one's reputation or in part from the motive of duty or to avoid punishment or disapproval within a religious community can deepen in becoming more purely responsive to those loved. In another way the depth of love's response to the needs of others increases as the measure and sensitivity of the love given increases. Another way in which religious love can deepen is through a change in consciousness of the kind that was discussed in the previous chapter. Coming to see the distant stranger or the beings of the earth in a new way that moves one's heart so that one responds to them with love is an interior change, which at the same time widens the scope of love.

Within religious sensibilities found in various religious traditions there is another more fundamental way that the depth of religious love can deepen. It consists in a turning from self religiously understood. In all human *agape* there is a degree of denial of self in that *agape* is given altruistically without the requirement of return. The denial of self that *agapeistic* religious love includes

---

1   The Book of Common Prayer, Daily Morning Prayer: Rite II, Confession of Sin.

can increase from a lesser to a greater degree. In its greater degree it may be spoken of as a loss of self. St. Bernard of Clairvaux in his presentation of the fourth degree of love, as we saw in chapter 4, speaks of one's losing oneself "as though you did not exist," although he regards the fourth degree of love as barely attainable in a human life and then only for moments. For other Christian thinkers loss of self ideally can be part of a constant religious love. Jacob Boehme (1575–1624), who spoke of "break[ing] the 'I'" or the self, said, "Love hates the 'I' because the 'I' is a dead thing and [the two] cannot stand together." The love contemplated by Boehme is of "the divine ground in yourself by which you love God's wisdom and miracles, as well as your brothers." Boehme's identification of "the divine ground in yourself" as the primary object of love reflects his mystical leaning. He also recognized the love of one's "brothers," or neighbors, and elsewhere in the work from which we are quoting he prays that God will allow him "to recognize correctly that all men come from One, and therefore all are members, brothers and sisters, as a tree with its branches; that I am to love all of them as You, O dear God, loved and still love us."[2] This love of his neighbors, of the divine ground in himself, and of God and his wisdom and miracles is for Boehme a constant love to be striven toward, and for it to be attained the "I" must be "broken."

In this connection we might speak of love under the patterning aegis of God's love. Love's being under the aegis of God's love does not necessarily mean that there is a thought of God as love's end or goal or that love is pledged to God. Here Meister Eckhart's thought is helpful. For Eckhart if one "truly has God he has him everywhere," and then one's "intention" is toward God alone, and all things are "nothing but God," as we saw in chapter 6. Eckhart says this in his counsel on detachment and the possession of God. For Eckhart there is a loss of self in the dying to self of detachment. But the God one has in the "true possession of God" is not a God of "constant contemplation." Rather, Eckhart says that "one ought to have a God

---

2   Jacob Boehme, *The Way to Christ*, trans. Peter Erb (New York; Ramsey, NJ; and Toronto: Paulist Press, 1978), Third and Sixth Treatises, pp. 91 and 178. *The Way to Christ* was originally published in 1624.

who is present, a God who is far above the notions of men and of all created things."[3] Eckhart is not addressing love of God or neighbor in his counsel. Yet we can draw from his counsel the implication that though there is no thought of God, God being "above the notions of men," one's intention may yet be toward God in loving others, and if one loves others in detachment one's love will turn from self. For Eckhart all that one does and all that one loves is nothing but God if one "has God" in a spiritual appropriation of God that is distinct from a cognitive belief and faith.

Loving others for the sake of God is loving others under the aegis of God's love, as is loving oneself or God for the sake of God. It is love with a depth that is patterned by God's love. Earlier, in chapter 6, when we drew on Eckhart's thinking for an understanding of loving others for the sake of God, we saw that loving others for the sake of God does not mean not loving others for their own sake, but loving them in God after one "has God" in all things, including love of neighbor and of oneself. Integral to such a love of others for the sake of God or in God, or of oneself (when one loves oneself properly and so as one loves others) is a turning from self or self-concern, we now see; and such a turning from self, when it is a part of love, is within the inner dimension of love and its depth. As that depth begins to approach the ideal of uttermost love, there is a lessening of a sense of self, or concern with oneself, that itself approaches a loss of self. For Bernard, in the fourth degree of love there is a losing of oneself in a momentary "union" with God in which one "become[s] like God." This union, for which Bernard uses the mystical metaphors of a drop of water being dissolved in wine, a red-hot iron becoming indistinguishable from the glow of fire, and air being suffused with the light of the sun, is for Bernard only just attainable for human beings, and then only briefly. For Boehme and Eckhart the loss of self, understood more

---

3   Meister Eckhart, *Counsels on Discernment*, trans. Edmund Colledge, O.S.A., Counsel 6. "Of detachment and of the possession of God," in *Meister Eckhart: The Essential Sermons, Commentaries, Treatises, and Defense*, ed. Edmund Colledge O.S.A. and Bernard McGinn (New York; Ramsey, NJ; and Toronto: Paulist Press, 1981), pp. 252–53.

in terms of a loss of self-concern and a turning from self-will, is not such a momentary event. If Bernard is right, as long as the "entanglements of the flesh" hold human beings back a complete loss of self and the fourth degree of love are impossible or barely possible and a loss of self can be a part of only a distant ideal of religious love. If Eckhart is right, detachment and turning from self-concern is attainable in a religious life that overcomes those "entanglements of the flesh."

III. HYPERINTERIORITY

RELIGIOUS LOVE that is developed exclusively in the exterior dimension of overt action (which amounts to the practice of beneficence) is lacking in the essential complement of feeling. Religious love developed exclusively in the interior dimension of love is lacking in the essential complement of an overt, practical expression. If both sides of love are truly necessary for religious love, then neither of these forms is truly love. At best each would be a truncated hybrid of love. The infinite ideal of love calls for a deepening of the depth of religious love, but if religious love develops exclusively or disproportionately in its interior dimension there is the condition of hyperinteriority. In this section we will examine the implicit endorsement of hyperinteriority by two religious authors: Leo Tolstoy and St. Augustine.

Leo Tolstoy

The reflections of Leo Tolstoy's (1829–1910) on the true demands of Christianity provide an opportunity to examine this condition. Tolstoy opposed what he saw as a compromised Christianity that had come to terms with the world. He challenged the accepted worldly ways of gaining one's own ends and offered his view of true or genuine Christianity, which he believed was grounded in the teachings of Christ. Tolstoy gave little place to dogma and ritual. For him true Christianity is "within you" and requires an absolute ethical commitment to Christ's original teachings, as Tolstoy understood them. His concern was with attaining "divine perfection." Tolstoy said,

> Divine perfection is the asymptote of the human life, toward which
> it always tends and approaches, and which can be attained by it
> only at infinity.[4]

Tolstoy's metaphor of the asymptote is the same used in this book's discussion. His asymptote, though, is that of "divine perfection," not love. His
is an infinite ideal, traveled toward on an infinite road, but its endpoint is not
infinite love. Tolstoy does allow that the "Christian teaching of loving God
and serving Him" informs the infinite "path to perfection." However, the
"teaching," which is "Christ's teaching," Tolstoy sharply distinguishes from
a commandment to love. His point is not that one cannot love if one's "love"
is given purely as a response to a command (the point we explored in chapter
6). Rather, his point is that there is no commandment to love. In his words,
"the commandment of love is not a commandment in the strict sense of the
word, but an expression of the very essence of the teaching."[5]

There are commandments, he allows, but they are not the teaching, and
they are negative, telling us what not to do. In the Sermon on the Mount
(Mt. 5) he finds five such commandments, each an attainable expression of
an "ideal," which it reflects. The ideal of having no ill will against anyone has
as its attainable commandment, do not offend anyone with a word. The ideal
of complete chastity yields the commandment to abstain from fornication.
The ideal of not caring for the future yields the commandment not to swear
or promise. The ideal of making no use of violence (which corresponds to
Tolstoy's own teaching of nonviolence) yields the commandment not to repay
evil with evil. And the ideal of loving our enemies yields the commandment to
do no evil to our enemies. These commandments "fail to form a teaching" and
following them is only "one of the endless steps" on "the path to perfection,"

---

4   Leo Tolstoy, *The Kingdom of God Is Within You*, trans. Leo Wiener (New York:
Noonday Press, 1961), chap. IV, p. 101. *The Kingdom of God Is Within You* was originally
published in 1893.

5   Tolstoy, *The Kingdom of God Is Within You*, Chap. IV, pp. 103–4.

although, for Tolstoy, they have the virtue that they can be followed in "our time," even if their associated ideals cannot be attained.[6]

Tolstoy is especially dubious about a universal command to love our neighbors. Love must have an object, he irrefutably observes. But love of humanity is a misnomer, for, he says, as opposed to family, race, and nation, "humanity is not an object, but only a fiction." Moreover, he finds that there is a "weakening of the sentiment [of love] in proportion as the subject [that is, the object of love] is widened." Tolstoy's criticism of the love of humanity is directed against "the preachers of the positivist, communistic, socialist brotherhoods" in particular.[7] However, its application, if valid, has a wider application. (Tolstoy's point anticipates the related claim that Carlo Ginzburg would make about a century later in his "Killing a Chinese Mandarin: The Moral Implications of Distance," discussed in the previous chapter.)

Yet Tolstoy does give a subsidiary place to love of neighbor. At one point he recognizes "the love and service of our neighbor" when it is "in consequence of the Christian teaching of loving God and serving Him."[8] Tolstoy does not make it clear what a *positive* expression of love of neighbor "in consequence" of loving God would be, or, for that matter, what a positive expression of loving God would be. He is much more concerned with what Christianity or "a Christian's conscience" requires one not to do. Beyond what is forbidden by the five negative commandments he finds in the Sermon on the Mount he names other specific actions to be avoided, which it may be are entailed by the five negative commandments (although Tolstoy does not make this claim). For instance, "the promise of allegiance to any government ... is a direct renunciation of Christianity," he says. "A Christian does not quarrel with anyone" and "without murmuring bears violence," Tolstoy says. "All obligations of state"—and he names "the oath, the taxes, the courts," and "the

---

6   Tolstoy, *The Kingdom of God Is Within You*, Chap. IV, p. 104–5.

7   Tolstoy, *The Kingdom of God Is Within You*, chap. IV, pp. 107 and 109.

8   Tolstoy, *The Kingdom of God Is Within You*, chap. IV, p. 105.

army"—are "contrary to a Christian's conscience."[9] (He is clear that he sees states and governments as deeply involved in violence, especially in their military action and, in nineteenth-century Russia, in the treatment of peasants.) Tolstoy, like Friedrich Nietzsche (1844–1900), seems to see the essence of Christianity in a not-doing.[10] This is not to say that Tolstoy espoused social quiescence. He believed and predicted "that the time will come when all men shall be instructed by God," and there will be no more wars, armies, prisons, or gallows.[11] Such a change for him will come, however, through a spreading embrace of negative action, as men (and women) refuse to condone violence, take oaths, pay taxes, and so on.

Although not paying taxes and avoiding court service (as a juror) and military service may involve one's taking action, Tolstoy does not tell us what positive steps there are among the "endless steps" on "the path to perfection." He does not tell us that responding compassionately to the needs of others is one of these steps or a requirement of the love of neighbor. He does not tell us that we may love God through loving our neighbors. When he allows that one may love one's neighbors "in consequence" of a love of God, he may mean that our neighbors may be loved for the sake of God, although he does not say so. If he means this, then the question of how he understands "for the sake of God" would arise. (And there are different ways of understanding this religious category, as we saw in chapter 6.) Perhaps he would allow that

---

9   Tolstoy, *The Kingdom of God Is Within You*, chap. IX, pp. 218, 220, and 236.

10   Nietzsche said that "genuine original Christianity" was not "a faith, but a doing: above all a *not* doing of many things," and in a clear but unacknowledged reference to the Sermon on the Mount he names for the most part the same things that are not to be done as Tolstoy. Friedrich Nietzsche, *The Antichrist*, in *The Portable Nietzsche*, trans. Walter Kaufmann (New York: Viking, 1954), pp. 606–7 and 613 (emphasis in the original). *The Antichrist* was written in 1888 and published in 1895. While Nietzsche wrote *The Antichrist* before the publication of Tolstoy's *The Kingdom of God Is Within You*, Nietzsche may have been acquainted with Tolstoy's *My Religion*, published in 1884, in which Tolstoy also found in the Sermon on the Mount five negative commandments.

11   Tolstoy, *The Kingdom of God Is Within You*, Chap. XI, p. 284.

loving neighbors for the sake of God can be done though neighbors are also loved for their own sake. But he does not say so, and he does not clearly reject Anders Nygren's view that human beings in themselves have no worth and in themselves are not worthy of love. Tolstoy is clear that violence and more are to be rejected, but it may be, for Tolstoy, for the sake of and in service to the "teaching."

Tolstoy says that "Christ's teaching . . . guides men, not by external rules, but by the internal consciousness of the possibility of attaining divine perfection." Christ's teaching, he says, "demands full perfection," that is, "the blending of God's essence, which abides in the soul of every man, with the will of God."[12] The religious idea that one must abandon one's self-will and make one's will the will of God is well recognized in the Christian tradition. Yet when Tolstoy fills the idea out in terms of a not-doing, he makes the practical end of religious striving a new consciousness or conscience without love's positive actions. Such a consciousness or conscience is not like the widening consciousness we examined in the previous chapter, for that consciousness has a positive active side. Tolstoy may not reduce love of God to a "state of mind" in the way, in chapter 2, we saw that Robert Solomon reduces romantic love to an "emotional process" or "state of mind," for it is "loving God and serving Him" that is the "Christian teaching" for Tolstoy, and as love *of* God loving God is essentially relational. Nevertheless by emphasizing a not-doing as the way of serving God, Tolstoy discounts the active side of love.

St. Augustine

As in Tolstoy's case, hyperinteriority can lead to a stress on the feelings of love—Tolstoy's Christian "conscience"—to the exclusion of positive action. There is another possible effect or form of hyperinteriority. St. Augustine was very much aware of the inner dimension of religious life, as are many. At one point, though, he does more than recognize the necessity and importance

---

12   Tolstoy, *The Kingdom of God is Within You*, Chap. IV, p. 102.

of its inner dimension. Reflecting on Jesus' teaching that we are to offer the other cheek if we are struck on the right cheek (Mt. 5.39) and on essentially the same teaching in Luke (Lk. 6.29), he states that

> these precepts refer rather to the interior disposition of the heart than to the act which appears exteriorly, and they enjoin on us to preserve patience and kindly feeling in the hidden places of the soul, revealing them openly when it seems likely to be beneficial to those whose welfare we seek.

Jesus himself, Augustine argues, did not offer the other cheek when he was struck (Jn. 18.23).[13]

What matters most, Augustine perceives, is the "interior disposition." But the lesson he presents is more radical than this. It is that the interior disposition, if maintained, allows any exterior act. We are to maintain patience and "kindly feelings," but if they are maintained, then "even war will not be waged without kindness."[14] Unlike many Christians in the first centuries of the Common Era, and unlike Tolstoy, Augustine sees no incompatibility between the teachings of Christianity and the violence of war. He insists, to be sure, that war be waged with kindness, but if that inner disposition is in place he thinks that any exterior act is permissible.

What Augustine's hyperinteriority does not allow him to see is that on the face of it and practically, certain actions are not compatible with feelings of kindness. There is no torture inflicted with kindly feelings toward the victim. Starving captives or refugees cannot be done with kindness.[15]

It is true that Augustine is not addressing the inner and outer dimensions of love, but of kindness. However, kindness is closely related to love.

---

13   St. Augustine, Letter 138, in *Saint Augustine, Letters 131–164*, trans. Sister Wilfrid Parsons, S.N.D., Writings of Saint Augustine, vol. 11 (New York: Fathers of the Church, 1953), p. 45.

14   St. Augustine, Letter 138, pp. 46–47.

15   In the thirteenth century and later, the Inquisition tortured heretics in order to bring them to renounce their heretical beliefs; the inquisitors did so in part to save others who might follow their heresies, but also to save the heretics themselves from eternal

(Kindness, as we will see in the following chapter, is seen by the Dalai Lama as a part of the greater connotation of compassion or "love and compassion" and, along with love and compassion, is included by John Hick in what he sees as "the basic ethical principle" of all the great religious traditions.) Augustine's thinking about the interior disposition of kindness and the exterior actions it allows clearly can be extended to the interior feelings of love and the exterior actions they would allow. What Augustine's form of hyperinteriority wrongfully denies is the essential *connection* of love's feelings with an exterior expression of that love. It is not only that love, and especially religious love, necessarily has both an interior and an exterior dimension; moreover the interior feelings of love are essentially connected to the loving actions that flow from those feelings.

---

damnation. It took the special belief that those who die professing a heresy will be eternally damned to begin to regard such tortures as being for the good or welfare of those tortured.

Chapter Ten

The Asymptote of Love

I. INTRODUCTION

THE ASYMPTOTE OF LOVE approaches the endpoint of infinite love, God's love in theistic religions. The asymptote of love, however, is the asymptote of human love, from which it proceeds. God's love, then, is human love raised to a more-than-human highest. In religious or Christian understanding, God's divine love as *agape* is human *agape* raised to the infinite. Following St. Thomas Aquinas, we may dimly understand God's love through an extrapolation from human love.

We can understand that God's love is *agapeistic*, given generously and utterly without condition. We can understand that it is compassionate love for those in suffering or in need. And we can understand that it is withheld from none. What is beyond human understanding is its infinite nature and the mysterious way in which it may be manifested.

God's love can be imaged and experienced, and as will be contended in section II, for a viable religious sensibility it can be manifested in human action. Also God's love can be emulated or imitated. It is followed in emulation when God is loved by following his command to love, for God's love is the perfect expression of the love he commands. And it is followed in imitation when Christians seek to imitate Christ's love. This means that God's love can be an ideal—not a human ideal, but an infinite, divine ideal—to be striven toward in human life. The role of the endpoint of the asymptote of love as an ideal of love will be turned to in the following section.

In section III, we will turn to an issue that affects the way the defining circumference of the circle of love is to be understood. It is the question of

139

the relation between love and compassion. We have spoken of love and compassion together, but they are not the same. Love as *agape* has a home in the theistic tradition of Christianity. Compassion has more of a home in the Buddhist tradition. Might the religious love that approaches uttermost love be just as well conceived of as compassion, following the direction of Buddhist thought? Love and compassion differ, but as we will see they also interdigitate and finally are pleached.

In section IV, we will take up another question that was asked at the end of chapter 2: Is uttermost love or the religious love that begins to approach it rational or reasonable? However, we will revise the question so that it becomes one of love's appropriateness and so better applies to religious love.

In section V, we will consider an issue that is closely related to the question of the appropriateness of religious love, but on which religious sensibilities are divided. Is the religious love that is to be given to neighbors and even to the nonhuman beings of the earth to be given though it is undeserved, or is it to be given as it is deserved?

The final section, VI, will provide an opportunity for a summary of the themes and concerns of this books' discussion. In the final section we will as well recognize a paradox that would arise for religious love if *per impossibile* it were to reach the endpoint of the asymptote of love.

II. GOD'S LOVE: THE ENDPOINT OF THE ASYMPTOTE OF LOVE AS THE IDEAL OF LOVE

THE IDEA OF AN INFINITELY HIGH IDEAL that guides action and aspiration is not foreign to either religious or philosophical reflection. When St. Thomas Aquinas presented God's love as "analogous" to but higher in an eminent degree than human love, he did not present God's love as an ideal for human aspiration. Yet such a role is implicit in his account.

God's love as the endpoint of the asymptote of love is infinitely remote and though approachable never fully attainable or even fully comprehendible. This, however, does not preclude its functioning as an ideal. Leo Tolstoy, who understood "divine perfection" as such an ideal, spoke of an "infinite road to perfection."[1] The road is traveled but by its nature not to its end. St. Bernard of Clairvaux had a similar idea regarding the affection of love, as we saw in chapter 5, for he allowed that human beings, through God's grace, can begin to have the sensation of love and even progress in that feeling, but he insisted that the command to have the feelings of love could not be completely fulfilled.

In the moral domain Immanuel Kant projected a similar picture when he postulated the endless progress of the moral will toward perfect agreement with the moral law—something that can occur only with an "endless duration" of human persons, Kant reasoned, and which led him to postulate the immortality of the soul.[2] Tolstoy's ideal is religious (although it is not the ideal of love), and Kant's ideal is philosophical and moral. Both illustrate the concept of an infinite ideal.

In the theistic traditions of the West, the highest love is God's infinite love, and it is God's love that is the infinite ideal of love. As we have seen (in chapter 4, and especially in chapter 7), the religious may understand and experience God's love in terms of different images, such as that of Bridegroom, Mother Jesus, and Good Shepherd. God's love in times of trial and tribulations, for instance, may be experienced as the comfort given by a merciful Mother. Also God's love may be directly manifested in the world as God's creation. All he created he saw as good, we are told in the book of Genesis. As Sallie McFague said in reference to John 3.16, God loves the world. And that love may be felt in one form of religious experience daily and moment by moment. For this religious perspective or sensibility, God's love is endlessly and ubiquitously manifested in our daily experience. The religious experience of God's presence becomes the religious experience of God's steadfast love, as in the Psalms. This is the experience of the radiance of God's love.

---

1   Leo Tolstoy, *The Kingdom of God Is Within You*, trans. Leo Wiener (New York: Noonday Press, 1961), chap. IV, p. 104.

2   Immanuel Kant, *Critique of Practical Reason*, trans. T. K. Abbott (Amherst, NY: Prometheus Books, 1996), bk. II, chap. II, sec. 4 of I. Elements of Pure Practical Reason, pp. 147–50. The *Critique of Practical Reason* was first published in 1787.

But there is yet another way of experiencing God's love in another dimension of that love. We saw in chapter 3 that there is a religious sensibility that recognizes an implicit love of God through the love of neighbors, the love of others. Conversely, for a related or for that same sensibility, God's love may be manifested in human expressions of love and compassion. For this religious sensibility, God's love and mercy for human beings in physical or mental need is manifested in the loving actions of human beings. Even when God's love and mercy are manifested in the changing of a human heart, as it is quickened in love or sympathy, God's love for this religious sensibility may often work that change through the actions of human persons. This sensibility is informed by a verse in John's first letter: "if we love one another, God abides in us and his love is perfected in us" (1 Jn. 4.12).

God's love given expression through human actions is for this religious sensibility truly God's love and worthy of emulation. Is it God's love in its "eminent" form, to use Aquinas' term? It is not God's *direct* love, as expressed in his presence and celebrated in the Psalms. It is God's love indirectly expressed through human love. For the religious sensibility informed by the verse in John's first letter, it is God's love "perfected in us." As God's love it is love in its eminent and highest form, though it gains expression in human love, which for Aquinas is only "analogous" to the love that it nevertheless expresses. In chapter 8 we saw how human love relationships may provide a template for religious love. For Aquinas human love gives us some understanding of God's love. But moreover, for this religious sensibility, compassionate human love may embody God's love and help express, partially and indirectly, the infinite ideal of God's love.

Though an infinite ideal, it can be sought after and even approached. Yet God's love as uttermost love, the endpoint of the asymptote of love, is itself an infinitely remote ideal of love. Consequently, while it may be approached and even partially expressed in human love, in its full nature it is ever infinitely over the horizon of human endeavor and aspiration.

To be sought after in emulation or imitation as an ideal, God's love must to some extent be understood and expressible, not wholly, which may be impossible, but adequately to direct endeavor. Here both images of God's love and human expressions of love may have a role, and here biblical stories and parables can also play a role for those in the Jewish and Christian traditions, as in the Islamic tradition the Qur'an and *hadith* provide guidance and direction. Here as well in these and other traditions a religious consciousness of the scope and depth of a love that begins to approach God's uttermost love can have a role to play. Such a religious consciousness may have several sources, not all of which are distinctly religious, as we saw in chapter 8, although a paramount source for Christians is the life and teachings of Jesus. Other sources may be theological. St. Thomas Aquinas championed the dominion view of the relationship between human beings and the other beings of the earth. Yet when he asked whether God loves all things, he replied that "God loves all things. For all existing things, in so far as they exist, are good."[3] Aquinas does not cite Genesis 1.31, although he might have. In any case he lends theological recognition to the universal scope of God's love as uttermost love.

Beyond the scope of love, the ideal of God's love in order to give direction to aspiration must also give guidance to action and the interior dimension of the religious love to be striven toward. As was indicated in the introduction to this chapter, there is a religious understanding of God's love as *agape*, given without condition, compassionate, and withheld from none. This general but limited understanding is available to those within the Christian tradition, but also to those not in that tradition. For Christians these features of God's love are manifested in Christ's life, and Christ's life provides an ideal of love of God and neighbor to be approached in imitation. And for a religious sensibility informed by the spirit of 1 John 4.12—whether or not it is a distinctive Christian sensibility—the ideal of love can be expressed in the compassionate love one person gives to another.

Questions may arise, though, if the scope of love is seen to embrace the nonhuman beings of the earth. Are they to be loved as human neighbors are loved? As we have seen, the expression of religious love, *agape*, can take different forms in different human relationships. Religious love for nonhuman beings may then also take different expressions. Religious love for the living

---

3   St. Thomas Aquinas, *Summa Theologica*, I, q. 20, a. 2, in *Basic Writings of Saint Thomas Aquinas*, ed. Anton C. Pegis, vol. 1 (New York: Random House, 1945), p. 217.

beings of the earth may be in the form of respect for them, given in ways appropriate to their different species. Religious love for the nonliving beings of the earth may be in the form of a respect for the integrity of such entities, in accord with our earlier discussion. For St. Thomas Aquinas, as we saw in chapter 7, when "anyone loves another, he wills good to that other." More strongly, for Aquinas, "to love a thing *is* to will it good."[4] Willing the good of the living and nonliving beings of the earth in the form of respect would come under what amounts to Aquinas' definition of love.

JUST HERE, however, we may want to consider whether literally *all* existing things are to be loved or respected. Aquinas in the thirteenth century was not aware of pathogenic bacteria, the malaria parasite, or disease-causing viruses. But we are. Earlier, in chapter 6, it was suggested that one way for a contemporary to express *agape* as love of neighbors would be to work to alleviate the suffering from malaria by seeking to find a cure for malaria. Can we respect existing beings like the malaria parasite while trying to eliminate them? Aquinas both accepted the dominion view of the relationship between human beings and the other beings of the earth, and proclaimed God's love for all existing things, which then sets the ideal for human religious love. If we seek to eliminate malaria and the other terrible diseases of the world are we in effect accepting the dominion model? Perhaps not, for seeking to eliminate the diseases of the world is not tantamount to thinking that human beings can do as they will regarding all the beings of the earth. But, though we can recognize that trying to contain or eliminate disease is not the same as embracing the dominion view, can we seek to eliminate the malaria parasite and other pathogens compatibly with respect for all existing things?

Respect for the nonhuman beings of the earth is not expressed in the same way that love for our human neighbors is expressed. Compassionate love for our human neighbors is expressed in giving relief from their suffering, and one

---

4   St. Thomas Aquinas, *Summa Theologica*, I, q. 20, a. 3, in *Basic Writings of Saint Thomas Aquinas*, p. 219 (my emphasis).

crucial way to do this is to eliminate the diseases that cause suffering. Respect for even the malaria parasite is required, as Albert Schweitzer respected the lives of flies in his hospital in Lambaréné in West Africa. Schweitzer, though, was clear that when human life and welfare required it, Reverence for Life allowed the reluctant taking of other lives.[5]

Though some positive forms of respect for the nonhuman beings of the earth are easily recognized, such as improving the living conditions of farm animals and preserving forests and wetlands, in other cases what forms such respect might or must take at this point in the evolution of religious consciousness remains an open question. Is vegetarianism entailed? Are specific practices of environmentalism entailed, such as a curtailed urban use of water? Answers to these questions, which are both moral and religious, as well as answers to many others, may need to await a quickening of religious consciousness regarding both the perimeter of the circle of love and how those beings in an expanded circle deserve to be treated. However, this state of affairs is not that different from love of our human neighbors, where there are unresolved questions about, for instance, what economic just treatment of global neighbors entails.

III. LOVE AND COMPASSION

LOVE, *agape*, is central to Christianity. St. Paul expresses the essential place in Christianity of love when he says, "if I have all faith, so as to remove mountains, but have not love, I am nothing" (1 Cor. 13.2). It is love that is commanded in the two great commandments. Compassion (*karunā* in Sanskrit and Pali) is central to Buddhism. It was taught by the Buddha and is the informing virtue of the *bodhisattvas*. Love and compassion are different in that, while love may be for those in need, compassion always is—and typically compassion is for those in great need. A mother's love for her young child may in great part be compassionate love in response to his needs, but

---

5   Albert Schweitzer, *Out of My Life and Thought: An Autobiography*, trans. C. T. Campion (New York: Henry Holt and Company, 1949), pp. 159 and 234.

the young child's love for his mother is not a compassionate response to her needs, for although she may have needs, the child will have no understanding of them. Jesus has compassion for those in the crowds that come to hear him "because they were harassed and helpless, like sheep without a shepherd" (Mt. 9.36). (The Greek word in the New Testament that is translated as compassion is not *agape* but *splagchnizomai*.) Buddhist compassion is for all sentient beings in their suffering. In the New Testament compassion is for certain fellow humans in great need, while love is to be given to all. Even if the second commandment could be recast as "have compassion for your neighbor" the first could not be recast as "have compassion for God." God in the Christian tradition, and in the other Abrahamic traditions, as the Supreme Being, is perfect and transcendent, and is traditionally conceived as having no needs. Only occasionally are needs attributed to God. Immanuel Kant, who was not a traditional Christian, very near the end of the second part of *The Metaphysics of Morals* said, "One may say (in human terms) that God created rational beings as if it were from a need to have someone beside himself whom he could love, or by whom he could also be loved."[6] Kant, though, is allowing only that God's need may be spoken of "in human terms" and then only "as if" God had a need to love or to be loved.

Thus there is good reason for love being the central category in the Western theistic religions in which God loves and God is loved, while compassion is the central category in Buddhism in which the *buddhas* and *bodhisattvas* have compassion for sentient beings, and Buddhists and other human beings are called on to have compassion for sentient beings (but not for *buddhas* or *bodhisattvas*).

Nevertheless love and compassion are closely related. John Hick speaks of "Agape/Karuna" as constituting a single criterion or norm, and in his more inclusive formulation he sees "love, compassion, self-sacrificing concern for the good of others, generous kindness and forgiveness," the essence of the

---

6   Immanuel Kant, *The Metaphysics of Morals*, Part II, *The Metaphysical Principles of Virtue*, II The Methodology of Ethics, Conclusion: Religion as a Doctrine of Duties to God Lies Outside the Limits of Pure Moral Philosophy, 488, in *Immanuel Kant: Ethical Philosophy*, trans. James W. Ellington (Indianapolis, IN: Hackett, 1983), bk. II, p. 159.

Golden Rule, as "the basic ethical principle of the great traditions."[7] The Dalai Lama observes that the Tibetan *nying je*, which is generally translated as compassion, in its greater connotation, includes "love, affection, kindness, gentleness, generosity of spirit, and warm-heartedness," as well as "sympathy" and "endearment."[8] Although the Dalai Lama includes kindness, generosity, and related virtues in the greater meaning of *nying je*, as John Hick includes kindness, generosity, and related virtues in Agape/Karuna, the Dalai Lama proceeds to speak of *nying je* as "love and compassion" (with its origins in "empathy").[9] For both Hick and the Dalai Lama there is a clear perception of the consanguinity of love and compassion and of their being compatible and capable of being combined, as they are in the Tibetan Buddhist concept of *nying je* for the Dalai Lama and in the "basic ethical principle" of all the great religious traditions for Hick.

The closeness of love and compassion in the Christian tradition becomes evident when we reflect that the parable of the Good Samaritan, which Jesus uses to show what it means to be a neighbor and to love our neighbors, presents the Samaritan as moved by compassion (*splagchnizomai*) for the man set upon by robbers (Lk. 10.33). It may be that the best way to understand the relationship between love and compassion is that love expresses itself as compassion, and is compassion, when given to those who are seen to be in great need or suffering. In the Buddhist tradition, in which all sentient beings are seen to be in unavoidable suffering (*duhka* in Sanskrit and *dukkha* in Pali), love is expressed in compassion. In the Christian tradition love, when it is love for God, is not compassion, but when it is God's love for his children and our love for our neighbors in their need it is compassionate love. We may appropriately speak of the endpoint of the asymptote of love, when it is compassionately given to those in need, as love/compassion.

---

7   John Hick, *An Interpretation of Religion: Human Responses to the Transcendent*, 2nd ed. (New Haven CT and London: Yale University Press, 2004), pp. 316 and 325.

8   His Holiness the Dalai Lama, *Ethics for the New Millennium* (New York: Riverhead Books, 1999), p. 73.

9   His Holiness the Dalai Lama, *Ethics for the New Millennium*, p. 74.

IV. THE APPROPRIATENESS OF LOVE

THE ISSUE OF the rationality or reasonableness of love, of religious love, may seem far from a religious concern. Martin Luther (1483–1546) saw reason as the enemy of faith, but, on the other hand, as we observed in chapter 4, St. Thomas Aquinas endeavored to show that reason and faith are not in conflict. The relationships between faith and reason, then, has been viewed differently by different theological traditions. Our concern, however, is with the rationality or reasonableness of religious love, not faith. If religious faith can seem far from reason, religious love may seem farther yet from reason. But there is another factor: the time in which we live. We live in an age in which the relevance of rationality is widely proclaimed. Perhaps rationality, at least in its practical applications, has always been given importance. Today, though, the importance of rationality can hardly be denied.

In chapter 2 we saw how David Hume regarded love as not answerable to reason and in this sense never contrary to reason or irrational. We also saw how if we understand rationality in terms of one's own self-interest, transactional love relationships might or might not be rational, depending on the negotiated terms of such a relationship. But *agape* (or love/compassion, as we may now understand it) in its approach to uttermost love is not of this character. *Agape* responds to those loved, and it is not given for the sake of love in return. Can such love be rational or reasonable?

Such a question, despite the concerns of our age, may not be deemed important by those who seek to love *agapeistically* and hence may not be pursued by them. Nevertheless reflection can be brought to bear on the question. In chapter 2 we briefly introduced the idea of redirecting the issue of rationality or reasonableness, making it a question about appropriateness. Reasonable dress for a wedding guest is appropriate dress, we observed. Let us now develop further the construction of appropriateness as a measure of what is reasonable in various instances or as a category in its own right.

Reasonable dress is to a great extent culturally determined. Reasonable highway speed can vary with road conditions. In other instances, though, what is reasonable in the sense of appropriate does not have this variability. Consider what has appropriateness because it is healthy or conducive to good health. True, what is healthy and invigorating for one person might in some cases be unhealthy for another person. Vigorous exercise may be like this. But other things are unhealthy for all. Tossing off half a glass of an arsenic compound is for each and all unhealthy, just as an intake of nourishing food is healthy for each and all. Arsenic is invariably inappropriate for human consumption, just as nourishing food is invariably appropriate for human consumption.

What is reasonable in the sense of being appropriate is fitting, and when the appropriateness is invariable because of the nature for which it is appropriate—as with appropriate food for humans—the fittingness may be said to be natural. *Agape* when it is love for persons is a response to persons. *Agape* for an identifiable religious understanding and sensibility is seen as a fitting response to persons because of their inherent worth. *Agape* would then be the attitude and way of treatment that human beings deserve because of their inherent worth. Given this nature of human beings as persons with inherent worth the appropriate, reasonable, and fitting response to them is *agapeistic* love, or *agapeistic* love/compassion, in some manifestation. This of course is not to say that this is the universal response of human beings to one another, only that it would be the appropriate response. Its being the appropriate response is in accord with the Christian and Jewish sensibility that finds the stranger to be in the image of God and to be one's brother or sister, and it accords with a central Buddhist sensibility. Coming to see one's fellow human beings as deserving one's love/compassion may require the change of perception, with a concomitant change in feeling, that we have identified. Nevertheless, although a change of heart in the religious sense may be involved, resulting in a new religious sensibility, it need not be a religiously inspired new perception occurring within an explicit religious allegiance, All that is necessary is the perception that human beings by their nature deserve a response of love or love/compassion.

This rationale, furthermore, is applicable to an expanded circle of love. Schweitzer's reverence for life would be rational or reasonable in the sense of appropriate if the living beings of the earth have their own inherent or intrinsic worth deserving of respect, as would Buddhist compassion for all sentient being if sentient beings have such intrinsic worth. And if this rationale is applicable to human beings and to the living things of the earth, it is applicable as well to the nonliving natural beings of the earth—mountains, deserts, prairies, and the like—if they too have an intrinsic worth that calls for respect.

V. LOVE AS DESERVED

CLOSELY RELATED TO THE QUESTION of the appropriateness of religious love, or love/compassion, is the question of whether religious love is to be given as deserved. The questions are so closely related that the one may be a paraphrase of the other. Yet as an issue about love being deserved it elicits divided religious intuitions.

St. Bernard of Clairvaux, as we saw in chapter 4, makes an argument that God deserves our love because he loved us first. Bernard goes on to augment this argument. Referring to "unbelievers," he provides additional reasons. "God," he says, "is always able to make their ingratitude plain by the innumerable kindnesses he showers on men for their benefit and which are quite obviously his gifts." Chief among these are "bread, sun, and air" and also beyond "bodily necessities" the "higher goods" of the soul: "dignity"—construed by Bernard as free will and also "the power of dominion" over all living things (the dominion view of the relationship between human beings and the other beings of the earth that was discussed in chapter 8)—"knowledge," and "virtue."[10]

Bernard does not discuss whether God's love is given to human beings, or the other beings of the earth, as it is deserved. He is clear, though, that God's love is *agape*, "love of one who wants nothing for himself," in accord with 1 Cor. 13.5, which is cited.[11] Bernard is also clear that God's love is not withheld from anyone. In the Christian tradition God loves even sinners.

---

10   St. Bernard of Clairvaux, *On Loving God*, in *Bernard of Clairvaux: Selected Works*, trans. Gillian R. Evans (New York and Mahwah, NJ: Paulist Press, 1987), pp. 175 and 176.

11   St. Bernard of Clairvaux, *On Loving God*, p. 175.

Are all those God loves, including sinners, deserving of his love? Bernard does not say. Regarding God's love for human beings, in Bernard's Christian tradition at least two answers are available, each correlating with a distinct religious sensibility. One is that human beings do not deserve God's love, but it is given nevertheless. The other is that human beings, though sinners, as God's children deserve the love of their Father, or, following Julian of Norwich, their Mother.

The first answer is subscribed to by Anders Nygren. Nygren, who holds that the "man who is loved by God has no value in himself" (as we noted in chapter 3), affirms that "God does not love that which is already in itself worthy of love." If God were to love in this way his love would be "legalistic," Nygren thinks. Rather, God gives his love freely and spontaneously. The only answer to the question "Why does God love?" for Nygren is "Because it is his nature to love."[12]

The second answer affirms the inherent worth of those God loves in accord with Jesus telling us that not even a sparrow falls to earth without God's will and then saying, "Fear not therefore; you are of more value than many sparrows" (Mt. 10. 31). For this answer God loves all the beings he created because he created them all deserving love in their nature. The second answer is also implicit in the thinking of St. Thomas Aquinas. Aquinas, as we observed earlier in this chapter, affirms that God loves all things. In reply to the question of whether God loves all things equally, Aquinas says that in one way he does and in another way he does not. He loves all equally in one way in that he loves all things by an act of will that is the same. But in another way "God loves better things more." Aquinas' thinking is this: to love a thing is to will it good, and since some things are better than others obviously God wills "a greater good for one than for another," which is to say God loves one more than the other.[13]

---

12   Anders Nygren, *Agape and Eros*, trans. Philip S. Watson (New York: Harper & Row, 1969), pp. 74–75 and 78.

13   St. Thomas Aquinas, *Summa Theologica*, I, q. 20, aa. 3 and 4, in *Basic Writings of Saint Thomas Aquinas*, vol. 1, pp. 219 and 220.

Aquinas does not directly address the question of whether God loves as deserved. As we saw earlier, Aquinas says that God loves all existing things and does so because all existing things "are good." If he would allow that those things created good deserve to be loved, then he would conclude not only that God loves all beings but that God has created them deserving love and accordingly loves them, and equally in the first way Aquinas identifies. Furthermore Aquinas can as much as Nygren recognize that it is God's nature to love, as he does in his way when he recognizes that "love exists in God."[14] That God loves by his nature may be affirmed by each of the two religious sensibilities that diverge on whether God loves as deserved.

A concern with giving love as deserved is not limited to religion. We find it also in Aristotle's treatment of the love of friendship (*philia*) in the *Nichomachean Ethics*. In chapter 1 in our introduction of *philia* (along with *eros*, *storge*, and *agape*) we referred to Aristotle's discussion of *philia* in the *Nichomachean Ethics*. Here we should heed his comments on giving the love of perfect friendship only as it is deserved. Aristotle identifies three main kinds of friendship. One is based on utility or mutual usefulness, as in business friendships; another is based on pleasure, as in a boyfriend-girlfriend relationship. The third kind of friendship, which Aristotle regards as perfect friendship, is between those who are "good in themselves." In this kind of friendship each "loves the other for what he is," as opposed to the usefulness or any pleasure to be obtained, although such friends might be useful to one another and be pleasing to one another. It is perhaps this kind of friendship that Aristotle has in mind when he says that "friendship seems to consist more in giving than in receiving affection." In a perfect friendship each deserves the affection he receives (or she receives, although Aristotle, in keeping with the time in which he lived, seems to consider perfect friendship to be between men). In perfect friendship the friends are similar in their goodness, but if there is a friendship between unequals, as there can be for Aristotle, "the better person must be loved more than he loves." Moreover, in forming a perfect friendship

---

14   St. Thomas Aquinas, *Summa Theologica*, I, q. 20, a. 1, in *Basic Writings of Saint Thomas Aquinas*, vol. 1, pp. 215–17.

"one man [cannot] accept the other, or the two become friends, until each has proved to the other that he is worthy of love."[15]

There is a difference between Aristotle's understanding of the giving of love (*philia*) and the religious understanding of the giving of love *(agape* or love/compassion) that is foundational to both the religious sensibilities before us (the sensibility that human beings do not deserve love but are loved by God and are to be loved by their neighbors nevertheless, and the sensibility that human beings deserve love). For Aristotle the love of perfect friendship is properly held back until the prospective friends have proven themselves worthy. For both religious sensibilities religious love for others is spontaneous and freely given. For one sensibility this is because the love that is commanded is to be given without hesitation even though it is not deserved. For the other sensibility it is because all deserve the love that is commanded. For each there is no place for deliberation on anyone's worthiness for love. For each, for different reasons, the question of worthiness does not and cannot arise. For each the love to be given emulates the ideal of God's love, which is itself spontaneous and freely given. And each allows that the love given to neighbors is for the sake of God, although only one allows that it is as well for the sake of the neighbor or in response to the neighbor who deserves love.

For Aquinas God created all that exists as good and God loves all that he created as good; by extrapolation we can say, beyond what Aquinas explicitly says, that he loves what deserves to be loved. Furthermore this would mean that God's universal love is appropriate for human beings and all existing things. From this we can infer that it is also appropriate for human beings to love existing things. In the light of our discussion of the relation between rationality or reasonableness and appropriateness in the preceding section such love is rational or reasonable in the relevant sense of being appropriate. A *concern* with whether love is deserved, like a concern with rationality, is felt by many of the religious, though not all, to be foreign to religion. These concerns might

---

15   Aristotle, *Nichomachean Ethics*, bk. VIII, chaps, 3, 7, and 8, 1156a6–56b32, 1158b25, and 1159a26, in *The Ethics of Aristotle*, trans. J. A. K. Thomson, revised by Hugh Tredennick (New York: Penguin Books, 1955), pp. 261–64, 270, and 271.

be felt to be especially foreign to a response of *agape* to others. And indeed a concern with whether love is deserved or a concern with whether one's love will be given rationally—with the required effort to identify the worthiness of love in the one to be loved—are foreign to the spontaneous character of *agape*, for if love is held back until the individual worth of the one to be loved is assessed, then love is made contingent on the confirmation of the worth of the one to be loved. Doing this would make loving religiously like the contingent giving of love in perfect friendship as Aristotle understood it and would make love "legalistic" in Nygren's sense. Also a concern with rationality and whether love is deserved may suggest that some deserve love and some do not. But these are features of endeavors to assess whether persons deserve love; they do not relate to the perception or sense that persons deserve love per se. If the religious perception that persons deserve love, which for many lies behind and is implicit in the command to love neighbors universally, is correct, no such deliberative weighing or sorting is called for or can have any role to play in the giving of love: the universal love of neighbors is appropriate as well as required, for all universally and without exception deserve to be loved. This religious perception, with a widened redirection, is also applicable to an expanded circle of love.

To be sure even if one who does not love becomes convinced through reasoning like that of Aquinas, or any reasoning, that love of neighbors and of the beings of the earth is deserved and appropriate, love itself may not follow for the reasons we saw in chapter 4. Here, though the task has been only to explore the deserving issue and establish that for one religious sensibility not only love of God but love of neighbor, and with an expanded circle of love, love of all the beings of the earth, is deserved by them.

VI. A RETROSPECTIVE LOOK AT THEMES AND CONCERNS TREATED IN THIS BOOK, AND A PARADOX

THE OVERARCHING THEME of this book is the uttermost love that is at the infinite endpoint of the asymptote of love. Included within or along with this theme are the themes of love of others or neighbors (chapter 3), love of God (chapter 6) and self-love, the proper self-love with which one should love oneself as one loves one's neighbors (chapter 2). These are forms of human religious love. Another major theme is God's love and how it might be known (chapter 7 and this chapter). God's love, in a theistic understanding, is identical with the endpoint, while the forms of human religious love are along the asymptote in the approach to uttermost love.

Closely associated with these major themes are themes that reflect back on them. One such is the theme of loving God through loving others (chapter 3). Another is the theme of approaching a knowledge of God's love and of the requirements of love of God and love of neighbors by an extrapolation from human love relationships (chapters 7 and 8), and another is the theme of God's love as an infinite ideal, at once unattainable and giving directive guidance, as it does through its various expressions, including an expression in human acts of compassionate love (this chapter). Religious love is *agape* or *agapeistic*, and another theme is the responsive nature of religious love. Arguably all love is responsive, for, as all love is binary, it involves the one who gives love and the object of love to which the one giving love in some manner responds. *Agapeistic love*, or love/compassion—religious love as it approaches uttermost love—for a viable religious perspective responds *agapeistically* to God and to other persons, and with an expanded circle of love, to nonhuman beings of the earth. In all these cases religious love's response is to the intrinsic worth of God, human beings, and other beings. That love is such a response is not in accord with every religious sensibility, but it is in accord with sensibilities shared by many of the religious, Christians and those in other traditions; and for such sensibilities love is appropriate and deserved by God, humans, and the beings of the earth.

We started in chapter 1 with a wide-angle look at the forms and kinds of love. Our overarching concern with uttermost love and the asymptote of love relates to love in its very highest form, but we started with the perception that the human concept of love embraces every form of love from its uttermost expression to his seamy and selfish forms. This foundational step helped mark the distinctive and distinguishing character of that religious love that begins to approach uttermost love. This initial endeavor notwithstanding, it has not been our concern to define love. Indeed if love is a polythetic concept, as it seems to be, it will have no essentialist definition. In this regard our initial and preliminary effort was to explore and recognize love's plastic nature and its wide-ranging variants. Love can be divided into kinds or classes in more than one way. One of these divisions, dating from antiquity, recognizes *eros*, *philia*, *storge*, and *agape*, and though these categories are valid and were drawn on in our discussion, there are other possible typologies. Love, we found, or noted as what is evident to many, has an interior and an exterior dimension, and it invariably involves a relationship between the one who loves and that which is loved. In human interpersonal love relationships love can go both ways, and the relationship can be very rich in its expectations and expressions. This relational nature of love importantly holds for the religious love of God and of neighbors. Yet these important characteristics of love do not constitute an essentialist definition of love, for hate, jealousy, and understanding, for instance, also exhibit these characteristics.

Rather than being an elaboration of any essentialist definition of love, the concerns of this book parallel and connect to its love-related themes. Among the questions addressed in this book are the following: How can God's love be known? (chapter 7); Can there be a command to love? (chapter 5); Can love be a response to a duty or command? (chapter 6); How can there be religious self-love? (chapter 2); How are self-denial and loss of self related to *agape* or religious love? (chapters 2, 9, and this chapter); Does *agape* bestow value on what is loved or respond to others and their inherent value? (chapter 2 and this chapter); How is loving others for the sake of God to be understood? (chapter 6); How are knowledge of God and love of God related? (chapter 4); How are *agape* and *eros* related? (chapter 2); and How are *agape* and compassion related? (this chapter). It was a concern of this book to distinguish love from beneficence (chapter 5) and from hyperinteriority (chapter 9), just as it was to consider the alleged impossibility of loving distant strangers (chapter 8). The circle of love, along with the expansions of religious consciousness, was a particular concern (chapter 8). Another concern was to address the issue of the appropriateness of religious love and whether religious love is given as deserved (chapter 2 and this chapter).

Many if not all of these concerns about religious love are inveterate, and often inveterate concerns generate divergent views that are both historical and contemporaneously viable. We found such divergent views regarding, for instance, whether the feelings of love are within human control (chapter 5) and whether there can be human knowledge of God's love (chapter 7). In order to bring forward these different views, we consulted theologians and religious thinkers in the Christian and other traditions and, more basically, different religious sensibilities, which at other times we consulted for the sake of the perspective they provide. Religious sensibilities are internally related to religious views that are expressed in religious practice and self-understanding, and as such are very far from theoretical views, although they may animate or be correlated with different theological approaches to issues. Divergent religious sensibilities can express apparently incompatible views. When this happened we did not argue that one is right and one wrong, and sometimes looked for common ground between them or for ways they might complement each other.

IF THE ENDPOINT OF the asymptote of love is God's love, or is infinite love nontheistically conceived, it is both approachable by human understanding and beyond human understanding. It can be both as the infinite ideal of love.

As human love begins to approach uttermost love, will its character change? In a way it will, and its doing so presents us with a paradox. We have argued that love in all its forms, trivial or profound, is relational, having a subject who loves and an object that receives love. Love between persons is more significantly relational in that close human love relationships, *agapeistic* or not, involve or invite mutual understanding, expectations, and reciprocity as an elaboration of their basic subject-object structure. Religious love of God and of neighbor, of course, are also relational. Those who love God give their love *to* God, and those who love their neighbors give their love *to* their neighbors. Compassion is similarly relational. In the Christian parable the Samaritan's compassion is *for* the man set upon by robbers. Buddhist compassion is *for* all sentient beings.

In religious love and compassion, however, there is to be no distinction between oneself, who loves, and those loved. In Buddhism there is the doctrine of no-self, which recognizes that the self of personality ultimately is an illusion. And in a Christian understanding, as Søren Kierkegaard and Meister

Eckhart saw, in love of oneself and love of neighbor there is no distinction between oneself and one's neighbor. St. Bernard of Clairvaux goes so far as to intimate that at the fourth degree of love of God the distinction between oneself and God is lost, as a drop of water becomes indistinguishable from the wine in which it is dissolved.

In the progressive development of love, following the asymptote of love, as love begins to approach the endpoint of the asymptote a paradox of love emerges. The relational aspect of love necessary for love ceases to be necessary in the sense that, with a growing turning from self, though there is yet the one who loves and those who are loved, the distinction between them ceases to register or registers less and less. And finally if human love *per impossibile* were to reach the infinite love that is uttermost love, then, as St. Bernard envisioned, any distinction between the one who loves and what is loved is lost, and love having lost its relational quality at its zenith loses the nature of love. At love's zenith, which is God's love, love is, as Dionysius had it, beyond human conception.

BIBLIOGRAPHY

Adams, Robert Merrihew. "Involuntary Sins." In *The Philosopher's Annual*, vol. VIII, 1985, edited by Christopher J. Martin, Patrick Grim, and Patricia Athay, 1–29. Atascadero, CA: Ridgeway, 1987.

American Baptist *Policy Statement on Ecology* (2017), http://www.abc-usa.org/wp-content/uploads/2012/06/ecology.pdf.

Amore, Roy C., and Julia Ching. "The Buddhist Tradition." In *World Religions: Eastern Traditions*, 2nd ed., edited by Willard G. Oxtoby, 198–315. Oxford, UK and New York: Oxford University Press, 2002.

Anselm, St. "Proslogion." In *St. Anselm's Proslogion*, edited and translated by M. J. Charlesworth, 101–155. Notre Dame, IN, and London: University of Notre Dame Press, 1965.

Aquinas, St. Thomas. *Summa Theologica*. In *Basic Writings of Saint Thomas Aquinas*, 2 vols., edited by Anton C. Pegis. New York: Random House, 1945.

———. *Summa Theologica* II-II, q. 64, a 1. In *St Thomas Aquinas, Summa Theologiae*, vol. 38. Translated by Marcus Lefébure, O.P., 19–21. Cambridge, UK: Blackfriars in conjunction with McGraw-Hill, New York and Eyre & Spotiswoode, London, 1975.

———. *De veritate*. In St. Thomas Aquinas, *Truth*, 3 vols. Translated by James V. McGlynn, S.J. Indianapolis, IN and Cambridge, MA: Hackett, 1954.

Aristotle, *Nicomachean Ethics*. In *The Ethics of Aristotle: The Nicomachean Ethics*. Translated by J. A. K. Thomson and revised by Hugh Tredennick. New York: Penguin Books, 1976.

Arndt, Johann. *True Christianity.*In *Johann Arndt: True Christianity*. Translated by Peter Erb. New York; Ramsey, NJ; and Toronto: Paulist Press, 1979.

Augustine, St. *The City of God*. Translated by Marcus Dods. New York: Modern Library, 1950.

———. Letter 138. In *Saint Augustine, Letters 131–164, Writings of Saint Augustine*, vol. 11. Translated by Sister Wilfrid Parsons, S.N.D. New York: Fathers of the Church, 1953.

Bennett, Jonathan. *A Study of Spinoza's Ethics*. Indianapolis, IN: Hackett, 1984.

Bernard of Clairvaux. St. *On Loving God*. In *Bernard of Clairvaux: Selected Works*. Translated by Gillian R. Evans. New York and Mahwah, NJ: Paulist Press, 1987.

———. "Sermons on the Song of Songs." In *Bernard of Clairvaux: Selected Works*. Translated by Gillian R. Evans. New York and Mahwah, NJ: Paulist Press, 1987.

Cadoux, C. John. *The Early Christian Attitude to War*. New York: Seabury Press, 1982.

Calvin, John. *Institutes of the Christian Religion—1536*. In *John Calvin: Selections from His Writings*, edited by John Dillenberger, 267–317. N.p.: Scholars Press, 1975.

Clark, Ronald W. *The Life of Bertrand Russell*. New York: Alfred A. Knopf, 1976.

Cowdin, Daniel. "The Moral Status of Otherkind in Christian Ethics." In *Christianity and Ecology: Seeking the Well-Being of Earth and Humans*, edited by Dieter T. Hessel and Rosemary Radford Ruether, 261–90. Cambridge, MA: Harvard University Press, 2000.

Dalai Lama, His Holiness the. (Bstan-'dzin-rgya-mtsho, Dalai Lama XIV). *Ethics for the New Millennium*. New York: Riverhead Books, 1999.

Dionysius. *The Divine Names*, in *Pseudo-Dionysius: The Complete Works*. Translated by Colm Luibheid. New York and Mahwah, NJ: Paulist Press, 1987.

———. *The Mystical Theology. Dionysius the Areopagite*. Translated by C. E. Rolt. London: SPCK, 1940.

———. *The Mystical Theology. Pseudo-Dionysius: The Complete Works*. Translated by Colm Luibheid. New York and Mahwah, NJ: Paulist Press, 1987.

Dorff, Elliot N. *For the Love of God and People: A Philosophy of Jewish Law*. Philadelphia, PA: Jewish Publication Society, 2007.

Eckhart, Meister. *Counsels on Discernment*. In *Meister Eckhart: The Essential Sermons, Commentaries, Treatises, and Defense*, edited by Edmund

Colledge, O.S.A. and Bernard McGinn, 285–94. New York; Ramsey, NJ; and Toronto: Paulist Press, 1981.

———. "German Sermons." In *Meister Eckhart, Teacher and Preacher*, edited by Bernard McGinn. Translated by Frank Tobin, 239–345. New York; Mahwah, NJ; and Toronto: Paulist Press, 1986.

Francis de Sales, St. *Treatise on the Love of God*. Translated by Henry Benedict Mackey, O.S.B. Westport, CT: Greenwood Press, 1945.

Ginzburg, Carlo. "Killing a Chinese Mandarin: The Moral Implications of Distance." *Critical Inquiry* 21, no. 1 (Autumn 1994).

Grazer, Walter E. "Strategy for Environmental Engagement: Building a Catholic Constituency." In *Christianity and Ecology: Seeking the Well-Being of Earth and Humans*, edited by Dieter T. Hessel and Rosemary Radford Ruether, 578–87. Cambridge, MA: Harvard University Press, 2000.

Hick, John. *A Christian Theology of Religions: The Rainbow of Faiths*. Louisville, KY: Westminster John Knox Press, 1995.

———. *An Interpretation of Religion: Human Responses to the Transcendent*, 2nd ed. New Haven, CT and London: Yale University Press, 2004.

Hume, Davis. *A Treatise of Human Nature*. Edited by L. A. Selby-Bigge. Oxford, UK: Clarendon Press, 1888.

John Paul II, Pope. *The Ecological Crisis: A Common Responsibility*. World Day of Peace message, 1990.

Julian of Norwich, *Showings*. In *Julian of Norwich: Showings*. Translated by Edmund Colledge, O.S.A. New York; Ramsey, NJ; and Toronto: Paulist Press, 1978.

Kant, Immanuel. *Critique of Practical Reason*. Translated by T. K. Abbott. Amherst, NY: Prometheus Books, 1996.

———. *Critique of Pure Reason*. In *Immanuel Kant's Critique of Pure Reason*. Translated by Norman Kemp Smith. Boston, MA and New York: Bedford/ St. Martin's, 1965.

———. *Grounding for the Metaphysics of Morals*. In *Immanuel Kant: Ethical Philosophy*. Translated by James W. Ellington. Indianapolis, IN: Hackett, 1983.

———. *The Metaphysics of Morals*. In *Immanuel Kant: Ethical Philosophy*. Translated by James W. Ellington. Indianapolis, IN: Hackett, 1983.

Kellenberger, James. *Dying to Self and Detachment*. Farnham, UK and Burlington, VT: Ashgate, 2012.

———. *Relationship Morality*. University Park, PA: Pennsylvania State University Press, 1995.

Kierkegaard, Søren. *Fear and Trembling*. In *Fear and Trembling and Repetition*, edited and translated by Howard V. Hong and Edna H. Hong, 1–123. Princeton, NJ: Princeton University Press, 1983.

———. *Works of Love*. Edited and translated by Howard V. Hong and Edna H. Hong. Princeton, NJ: Princeton University Press, 1995.

Leopold, Aldo. *The Land Ethic* In *A Sand County Almanac*, enlarged edition. New York: Oxford University Press, 1966.

Lewis, C. S. *The Four Loves*. New York: Harcourt, Brace, and Company, 1960.

Mackie, J. L. "Evil and Omnipotence." In *God and Evil: Readings on the Theological Problem of Evil*, edited by Nelson Pike, 46–60. Englewood Cliffs, NJ: Prentice-Hall, 1964.

Malcolm, Norman. "Is It a Religious Belief that 'God Exists'?" In *Faith and the Philosophers*, edited by John Hick, 103–10. New York: St. Martin's, 1964.

Martin, Mike. *Love's Virtues*. Lawrence, KS: University Press of Kansas, 1996.

Matt, Daniel Chanan. Introduction to *Zohar: The Book of Enlightenment*. New York; Ramsey, NJ; and Toronto: Paulist Press, 1983.

McCloskey, H. J. "God and Evil." In *God and Evil: Readings on the Theological Problem of Evil*, edited by Nelson Pike, 61–84. Englewood Cliffs, NJ: Prentice-Hall, 1964.

McFague, Sallie. *Models of God: Theology for an Ecological, Nuclear Age*. Philadelphia, PA: Fortress Press, 1987.

Mill, John Stuart. *Utilitarianism*. Edited and introduction by George Sher. Indianapolis, IN: Hackett, 1979.

Montefiore, Hugh. *Can Man Survive?* London: Fontana, 1970.

Nammalvar. *Hymns for the Drowning: Poems for Vishnu by Nammalvar*. Translated by A. K. Ramanujan. Princeton, NJ: Princeton University Press, 1981.

Narayanan, Vasudha. "The Hindu Tradition." In *World Religions: Eastern Traditions*, 2nd ed., edited by Willard G. Oxtoby 12–125. Oxford, UK and New York: Oxford University Press, 2002.

National Council of Churches Open Letter. *God's Earth Is Sacred: An Open Letter to Church and Society in the United States* (2017). http://www.ncccusa.org/news/14.02.05theologicalstatement.htm.

Newman, John Henry. *An Essay in Aid of a Grammar of Assent*. Notre Dame, IN and London: University of Notre Dame Press, 1979.

Nietzsche, Friedrich. *The Antichrist*. In *The Portable Nietzsche*. Translated by Walter Kaufmann, 569–656. New York: Viking, 1954.

Nygren, Anders. *Agape and Eros*. Translated by Philip S. Watson. New York: Harper & Row, 1969.

Pascal, Blaise. *The Pensées*. Translated by J. M. Cohen. Harmondsworth, UK: Penguin Books, 1961.

Phillips. D. Z. "Faith, Scepticism, and Religious Understanding." In *Faith and Philosophical Enquiry*. New York: Schocken Books, 1971.

Plato. *Symposium*. In *The Collected Dialogues of Plato*, edited by Edith Hamilton and Huntington Cairns, 526–74. Translated by Michael Joyce. Princeton, NJ: Princeton University Press, 1963.

Runzo, Joseph. "Eros and Meaning in Life and Religion." In *The Meaning of Life in the World Religions*, edited by Joseph Runzo and Nancy M. Martin, 187–201. Oxford: Oneworld, 2000.

Russell, Bertrand. "My Mental Development." In *The Basic Writings of Bertrand Russell 1903–1959*, edited by Robert E. Egner and Lester E. Denonn, 37–50. New York: Simon and Schuster, 1961.

Singer, Irving. *The Modern World*, vol. 3. *The Nature of Love*. Chicago, IL: University of Chicago Press, 1987.

Smith, Adam. *The Theory of Moral Sentiments*, 6th ed., edited by Knud Haakonssen. Cambridge, UK: Cambridge University Press, 2002.

Soble, Alan. *The Philosophy of Sex and Love: An Introduction*. St. Paul, MN: Paragon House, 1998.

———. *The Structure of Love*. New Haven, CT: Yale University Press, 1990.

Solomon, Robert C. *About Love: Reinventing Romance for Our Times*. New York: Simon and Schuster, 1988.

Spinoza, Baruch. *Ethics.* In *Spinoza's Ethics*. Translated by Andrew Boyle. London: Dent and New York: Dutton, 1959.

Schweitzer, Albert. *Out of My Life and Thought: An Autobiography.* Translated by C. T. Campion. New York: Henry Holt and Company, 1949.

Talbott, Rick F. *Jesus, Paul, and Power.* Eugene, OR: Cascade Books, 2010.

Teresa of Ávila, St., *Way of Perfection.* In *Complete Works of St. Teresa.* Translated by E. Allison Peers. 3 vols. London: Sheed and Ward, 1972.

Thurman, Howard. *Disciplines of the Spirit.* New York; Evanston, IL; and London: Harper & Row, 1963.

Tolstoy, Leo. *The Kingdom of God Is Within You.*Translated by Leo Wiener. New York: Noonday Press, 1961.

Tugwell, Simon, O.P. *Ways of Imperfection: An Exploration of Christian Spirituality* Springfield, IL: Template Publishers, 1985.

Unamuno, Miguel de. "Saint Manuel Bueno, Martyr." In *Great Spanish Stories,* edited by Angel Flores. Translated by Anthony Kerrigan, 336–79. New York: Modern Library, 1956.

Weil, Simone. *Gravity and Grace.* Translated by Emma Crawford and Mario von der Ruhr. London and New York: Routledge, 1952.

INDEX